Cycling the Me

Cycling the Mediterranean

Bicycle Tours in Spain, France, Italy, Greece, and Beyond...

Kameel Nasr

Bicycle Books – San Francisco

Copyright © 1996 Kameel Nasr

Printed in U.S.A. by Data Reproductions

Published by:
Bicycle Books, Inc.
1282 - 7th Avenue
San Francisco, CA 94122
U.S.A.

Distributed to the book trade by:

U.S.A.:	National Book Network, Lanham, MD
U.K.:	Chris Lloyd Sales and Marketing Services, Poole, Dorset
Canada:	Raincoast Book Distribution, Vancouver, BC
Australia:	Tower Books, Frenches Forest, NSW
Sth. Africa:	Book Distributers International, Sandton

Cover design by Kent Lytle, Lytle Design, Alameda, CA

Maps by Eureka Cartography, Berkeley, CA

Index by Kish Indexing Service, Mendocino, CA

Frontispiece photo by Astrid Hansen; all other photos by the author

Publisher's Cataloging in Publication Data:
Nasr, Kameel B., 1949–
Cycling the Mediterranean: Bicycle Tours in Spain, France, Italy, Greece, and Beyond…
Series title: The Active Travel Series
Bibliography: p. Includes Index
1. Bicycles and bicycling, touring guides
2. Travel, Mediterranean
I. Title; II. Authorship
Library of Congress Catalog Card Number 95-83337
ISBN 0-933201-74-5 Paperback original

With special thanks to Joan Mersman

About the Author

Kameel B. Nasr was born in Lebanon and grew up in San Francisco. He has an M.A. from De Paul University, where he has also taught writing. Since then, he has worked as a journalist with an English-language newspaper in Jerusalem, and has written articles on travel and Middle East politics.

In 1980, he got on his bike and proceded to ride from San Francisco to Chicago. Since then, he has continued long-distance bicycle touring on a big scale, literally traveling around the world by bike, returning with enough stories to keep him writing for a while, but also with a mind full of questions about the values of modern society.

Although delighted to grapple with heavy religious and social issues, he keeps an open mind about the lighter side of life. He lives in a rural house in Italy and still regularly engages in bicycle tours, especially in his favorite region—the Mediterranean.

Table of Contents

Chapter 1
Introduction

The Mediterranean, one of the world's most beautiful areas, also happens to be one of the most accessible places for cycling. Rich with the history of Western civilization, the area has played host to numerous influential cultures, including those of the Athenians, Romans, Venetians, Israelites, and Egyptians.With its cozy ports and beaches, its cliffs and hills, its varied vegetation, fruits, and flowers, the Mediterranean provides the cyclist with a wonderful mixture of vistas.

The cultures of the countries that border the Mediterranean Sea share a history that has made them similar in their moral and family values, social ethics, and gastronomic tastes, and yet each region has preserved its own distinct character. For cyclists, this culturally rich area that includes southern Europe and the Middle East is a wonderful place to ride. Most roads are first rate, with a variety of terrain and plenty of opportunities for either solitude or crowds.

Overview map of the Mediterranean region. The countries included in this book are shown in color.

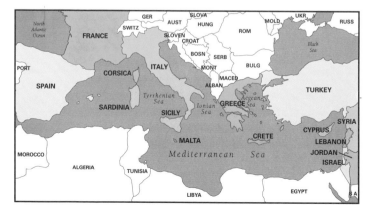

Climate

The rainy and cold season lasts from November to April and often makes winter too chilly to ride for most cyclists. Even spring sometimes requires cold-weather gear. Summers are hot and, with the exception of a brief and cooling cloudburst, dry. The Mediterranean Sea generally stays warm through the fall—the farther south, the longer it stays warm—but only becomes swimmable again as late as June.

The region has variable winds, but the major forceful wind patterns for the region come from the west and north. Summer usually has lighter breezes, but there are times when winds rip harshly for up to three days, generally from the west, and all you can do is hope you're riding in the same direction. Most coasts have a sea breeze. Generally, cyclists ride east and south, which tends to take advantage of the prevailing winds.

The best times to tour this region are late spring and early fall. Most cyclists take their Southern European tours in the summer, most likely for the convenience of being able to take off from school or work during that time. However, in summer the roads are quite crowded, especially during the month of August. This region has many more accidents during the summer because of the increased traffic, although many of these accidents occur at night when cyclists are not on the road.

I'm not trying to discourage summer tours—there's something to be said about being in a lively vacation crowd, and summer has the longest times of daylight—but perhaps I can suggest June or September as better months to travel. June has the benefit of more hours of daylight than other months, but autumn has the pleasant advantage of lower temperatures and fewer tourists. June and September also have fewer mosquitos. May and October are also fine, but be prepared for rain and the occasional chilly evening.

Cost

Prices for accommodation, air travel, ferries, and to some extent food depend on the season. For example, a ferry on Moby Lines from Livorno, Italy, to Olbia (Sardinia) costs 34,000 lire ($21) in the low season and 80,000 lire ($50) in the high season, August (1994 prices). Keep in mind that the more developed countries such as Italy will be more expensive than the moderately developed region of the Middle East, so prices will vary between countries.

Turkey and Syria are the least expensive places in the region, while Southern France, Italy, and Corsica can be quite pricey. Hotels can cost from $5 a night in Syria and Turkey to $1000 a night—seriously—in the exclusive resort hotels of the Riviera. Of course, most cyclists do not stay in such deluxe accomodations, and the majority prefer to camp at the many campgrounds costing about $4–12 per person per night. Restaurants can also vary widely in price range. In Italy you can eat a pizza for $5–8, but a full meal at a decent restaurant costs $15–25. In Greece a meal at a local taverna will cost $5–10. Grocery stores and supermarkets abound, so most cyclists on a budget buy supplies at these places and cook in a campground or eat along the road. Prepare to spend generally $15–25 a person a day during your tour for budget touring—and add the additional cost for hotel accommodation and restaurant meals if you are not.

Bring cash, traveler's checks, and credit cards if you have them. Keep your traveler's check stubs separate, and keep a record of your credit card numbers, as well as a photocopy of your passport, in case one of these gets lost. Some European cities have machines on the streets that will exchange foreign bills (though the rate is slightly less favorable than at most banks) or give you money from your credit card. Check for the best exchange rates, and try to avoid commissions when exchanging money. But don't waste too much time hunting for the best rate: if you're changing $100, there is only $0.60 difference between getting 130 or 131 Spanish pesetas to the dollar.

The Middle East

Some of our tours are in Middle Eastern countries. The Islamic culture that awaits you there may be unfamiliar, but it should not be intimidating. Yes, there is theft, religious fervour, and a strong military presence; but for the tourist, the Middle East is probably safer than Europe. No one is interested in harming a western tourist who stays away from illegal deals and honors the traditions of the country he or she is visiting. Don't miss a truly rewarding and fulfilling cycling experience because of prejudice.

As of this writing, the Middle East is in a state of flux, which may result in some positive changes for an often troubled area. The political situation notwithstanding, riding through the Arab countries is stimulating. In general, it's a noisy, friendly, talkative culture: when you ride into a village, everyone wants to wave at you, shake your hand, ask you questions. Expect to be offered hospitality constantly; in the countryside, you will find no reason to stay in a hotel or buy your own cup of tea.

Islamic countries expect conservative dress, especially in areas off the beaten track. It's fine to wear shorts while riding, but have long pants or a dress handy when you want to walk around. Cycling is becoming a popular sport among Arab men, so you can now find bicycle shops in every town. The shops won't be able to replace your derailleur, but they can repair your bike's broken parts. On the road, cars have priority, and bicycles must yield to them.

Packing

Be sure you know the essentials of bicycle touring before taking this or any other lengthy trip to a foreign country. Inform yourself about what equipment to take, how to pack your bicycle, safe and efficient riding techniques, medical considerations, and basic bicycle maintenance. This book assumes that you've been on at least one 3–5 day tour and concentrates on the routes in Southern Europe and the Middle East. If you do not have much touring experience, don't worry, since the Mediterranean is a good region for beginning cyclists as well as for veterans, but do consult books that give practical guidelines for the sport, and take short tours near home to get the hang of it. Generally, you should be able to ride at least 75 km (45 miles) a day without fatigue.

Generally, a touring bike is a better choice than a mountain bike, as almost all the roads described here are well asphalted. Use a mountain bike only if you're going off-road or intend to bicycle a lot in Turkey where some roads are less smooth.

Remember to travel light. If you are uncertain whether to take a particular item, leave it behind. Do bring spare tires and other essential spares, a basic bicycle repair kit, a pump, accurate maps, and bicycle clothing, and always carry a medical kit.

Legalities

Most borders in this area require no prior visas for Westerners. The exceptions are Syria, Jordan, and Lebanon, which require visas beforehand. Other countries where visas are required will stamp your passport on arrival. If you want to include Arab countries in your tour—and I highly recommend them for the friendliness of the people—you should contact the countries' consulates or tourist offices for their entry requirements. At current writing, Lebanon remains off-limits to most Americans. Consulates and tourist offices are also a good source of information about festivals and activities. Inoculations are not required in any of these countries unless you have recently been in a disease-infected area.

Americans can now receive travel information about particular countries as well as up-to-date entry requirements and advisories from their State Department via fax (fax number 1-202-647-3000).

Always be respectful of authorities: the rules of the host country are not always apparent. Be polite, unaggressive, and sociable, and you will have a much better time.

Safety

Unfortunately theft is a considerable problem in every country you will be visiting, even Malta and Cyprus, where not long ago people habitually left their doors unlocked. Use commonsense precautions: keep your bike and equipment securely stowed or within eye sight. Youth hostels in the large cities are terrible places to keep your things—you're almost guaranteed to be robbed if you leave your panniers under your bed. Campgrounds tend to be safer, but to be certain, ask someone responsible such as a hostel or campground director where you can safely store your bike and equipment.

Use a money belt while walking in the large cities, and have a strap on your handlebar bag so that you can take it off and use it as a shoulder bag. Your passport, airline tickets, wallet, traveler's checks, and credit cards should be kept with you at all times. Women traveling alone should expect some unwelcome attention, but with common sense all travelers can be safe.

Food and Drink

The love of eating unifies the diverse cultures of the Mediterranean, and all their cuisines are uniquely wonderful. Food stores, and especially open air markets when you stumble across them, have high-quality fruits, vegetables, breads, nuts, and other nutritious riding food. Most water in cities is drinkable, but to be safe, buy the readily available and inexpensive bottled water in stores.

Don't use drugs or excessive alcohol during your trip. All the countries covered in this book have strict anti-drug laws, and getting drunk is considered bad manners in any culture.

Sightseeing

Before leaving on your trip, think about your priorities. You will burn out in a few days if you try to visit every museum, every castle, every cathedral along the way. A well-rounded trip will include diverse activities, but don't try to cram. The interiors of castles, for example, are not that interesting after you have visited two or three. Go Mediterranean: relax, enjoy the people, the countryside, and the food in order to make the most of your vacation.

Most of the region observes a long lunch hour where the shops and tourist places close and everyone goes home, usually between 1:00 and 4:00 in the afternoon. Modern commercialism is seeking to eliminate this custom, but it is dying hard; the lunch hour remains sacred. Do your lunch shopping before the afternoon. Since it is also a hot time to ride, many cyclists plan to rest, go to the beach, or walk about town during that time. Cycle touring gives you independence from following a rigid schedule: go where you like and spend as much time as you wish in the areas that interest you.

One of the advantages of bicycle travel is meeting the inhabitants, so balance visits to the cathedrals or the Uffizi Gallery in Florence with conversations with native Italians, Arabs, and Greeks.

Nudists will find a whole range of suitable beaches in Spain, France (including Corsica), Italy (including Sicily and Sardinia), Greece, Israel, and Cyprus. Location and description of these places are available in *The World Guide to Nude Beaches and Recreation*, which is available in the U.S. from the American Sunbathing Association, tel. 1-800-879-6833.

Accomodations

Most European cyclists camp or stay at hostels. Camping places are abundant in Spain, France, Italy, and Greece, and are available to a lesser degree in the part of Turkey covered here, Israel, and the islands. Campers are usually a friendly crowd, and campgrounds are safe places. All countries have laws against do-it-yourself camping. Generally, never try camping by yourself on a beach or in an area you do not know.

Hostels are also wonderful places to stay, especially in Spain, France, and Italy. Membership in the International Youth Hostel Federation will provide you with a guide detailing the location of all hostels in Europe. In Greece a hostel is more like a dormitory where no Youth Hostel membership is required. Hostels are good places to meet people from around the world, to share stories and addresses. They cost $5–15 a night and are often located in a beautiful old building.

Hotels are tightly regulated and appraised by all governments, and they usually have their prices posted. In the areas we're traveling you will find all strata of accommodation. Even if you generally camp, spending a night every so often at a hotel, taking a hot bath and sleeping in a cozy bed, is a deserved reward for your hard work.

Post Office and Telephone

The post office and telephone systems are generally good in all the countries. Exceptions include the postal system in Italy and the telephone systems in Syria, Lebanon, and Jordan, which require that to make an international call you either telephone from a hotel, always more expensive, or go to a central station. In Spain, France, and Italy you can call overseas from a pay phone by buying a phone card. Intercontinental phone rates are much higher calling from Europe than from the U.S. Along the way, mail can be received either at a poste restante (general delivery) or, if you have bought American Express traveler's checks or have their card, at one of their offices.

In all the countries we are visiting except Cyprus the metric system is used, so to keep things simple we will use only kilometers: 1 km = 0.61 miles (about ⅝ mile).

Getting There and Around

Decide where you want to start. This tour starts arbitrarily at Rome and goes both west around the Mediterranean to the tip of Spain and east toward the Suez Canal and is designed so that you can start at any point and go in either direction, just by reading everything backward. Also included are some possible side trips.

Then shop around at travel agents for a good fare to and from your start and end point, get a box for your bike, take it apart, and put it on a plane. International flights usually accept a boxed bicycle and often an unboxed bicycle at no extra charge. During the tourist season you can find inexpensive charters from most European cities to the airports in the south such as Malaga, Almeria, Nice, Corsica, and many of the Greek islands. Most of these charters, however, must be booked from the country of origin, as they have no foreign representation.

Buses and trains are plentiful in the area and most accept bikes in the baggage car or underneath. Hitchhiking is not recommended since finding a car to stop is usually difficult. Air travel within the region is frightfully expensive, but if that is no objection, then it will be consoling to know that most European airlines will carry your bicycle without charge and the hassle associated with taking bikes on domestic airlines in the United States.

Much of the travel in the region is by ferry—not only to or between the islands, but also, for example, from Italy to Greece. The prices of ferries can vary quite a bit depending on the season, class, and the ship. The prices I have listed are rough estimates. For example, a ferry from Haifa to Pireas costs as little as $70 deck-class, but during the high season you can pay $150 for a bed. It is hard to obtain accurate information about ferries abroad, and ferry services change, so when planning to travel by ferry, keep your schedule slightly flexible.

Maps and Orientation

The sketch maps in this book are suitable for general orientation, and they should be supplemented with more detailed road maps. Generally, the most suitable maps for cycling can only be purchased locally. However, it is quite possible to make do with what can be readily purchased back home at large map stores, such as the Rand McNalley retail outlets in most main cities and specialty travel book stores. Any book store can order almost any map mentioned in this book from a map distributor such as MapLink, who also supplies directly to the consumer—see the Appendix for the address.

For overall route-planning, one map that shows the entire region or the country (or countries) you plan to visit is fine. A good overall regional map is Freytag & Berndt's *The Mediterranean* at scale 1:2,000,000 (i.e. 1 cm on the map represents 20 km in the terrain—or 1 in. represents 33 miles). Most major map publishers have individual country maps at a scale of about 1:1,000,000, which are suitable for advance planning of your tour. Another good source, especially if you will be visiting several countries, is the *Michelin Road Atlas of Europe*.

For cycling, the nicest maps tend to be the most detailed, and those are most easily obtained locally. Maps to scale 1:200,000, on which each cm represents 2 km in the terrain (1 in. represents 3.3 miles), are about the best for these tours, but for less densely populated regions, 1:400,000 or 1:500,000 is adequate.

The Routes

The book describes a series of routes following the coast as it passes famous areas—the Riviera, Athens, the Costa Brava, Sicily, the Holy Land, the ancient Greek cities in Asia Minor, Crete, Florence, and Damascus. Obviously, there are many more routes in Southern Europe and the Middle East than those given in the subsequent pages. These routes were selected for their combination of safety for cyclists, amount of traffic, closeness to accommodation, historical interest, degree of difficulty, and ease of connection to all areas around the Mediterranean. All these countries are mountainous once you move inland, so some roads can be difficult. But for the most part the tour can be taken by most people, young or old, in moderately good physical condition. The more challenging parts are described in more detail.

You can also integrate part of this tour with travel by car, and recently I saw two Italian couples who had a wonderful car-bike relay. One couple would take down their bikes and ride while the other couple would drive about 20 km, park near the road, and get out and bike. Then the first couple would arrive at the car, put their bikes on top, and drive and park about 20 km ahead. At night, they'd meet again at their destination for the day. They made time, saw the sights, and were not at all tired. It's one solution suitable for these two couples' situation, and with a bit of imagination, you'll probably come up with the way of traveling that works best for you.

Good riding. May your vacation be an adventure.

Chapter 2
Italy North of Rome

This chapter and the next describe two tours in Italy, both of which originate in Rome. The first tour, described in this chapter, travels north and west around the Riviera, and connects with the tour of France described in Chapter 4. The second tour, described in Chapter 3, goes south from Rome to Naples and either down the "boot," to connect with the tour of Sicily described in Chapter 16 in the soutwest, or across to Brindisi on the east coast, where it links up with the tour of Greece described in Chapter 6.

In addition to these tours on the Italian mainland, you will find some of the best bicycle touring on the two large Italian islands, Sicily and Sardinia. For a tour of Sardinia, see Chapter 15; for Sicily, see Chapter 16. From Sardinia, you can easily reach the French island of Corsica, also described in Chapter 15; and from Sicily, it's only a short hop to Malta, which is described in Chapter 12.

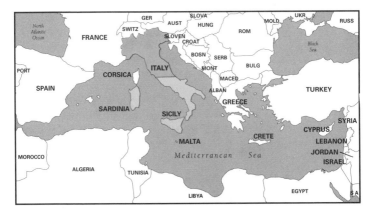

Cycling in Italy

It is difficult to find people who don't like Italy. Many writers have described the beauty of this country's lush green valleys, magnificent lakes, and active volcanoes. Almost as legendary is the contagious gregariousness of the people. Certainly, Italy encompasses a healthy share of Western history: it was here that modern art, music, and literature evolved and later spread to the rest of Europe. A third of the world's art, so claims the Italian tourist authority, sits in Italy.

Today's Italy, the world's fifth-largest economy, poses modern problems for overland travelers: chiefly traffic, pollution, and an increasing crime rate. The theft problem is strong particularly in the tourist areas of the large cities, but always err on the side of caution to be safe everywhere. The problem with traffic is mostly in the north, where Italy's narrow roads compound the congestion. Cycling is a popular sport in Italy, so most cars will give you ample space, but try to avoid the principal roads in the north, except on Sunday when trucks are prohibited from driving and many people take to the roads on their bikes.

As with all the tours described in this book, it is preferable to bring your own repair equipment and spare bicycle parts. Even in Italy, where cycling is popular, the cycling shops are not going to be an option when you're out in the countryside.

To find your way in Italy, there are two excellent series of maps. The first one is that published by the Italian automobile association at scale 1:300,000, available at many book and stationary shops, as well as at Auto Club Italia offices. The other series is the regional maps by Instituto Geografico d'Agostini at 1:250,000 (for this tour, you'll need sheets 2, 9, and 11). Both are readily available in larger book stores throughout Italy.

Finally, there is the Ravenstein (also known as RV) road atlas to Italy at scale 1:300,000—if you want to save weight, just tear out the relevant sheets to carry along. In the United States, most of these maps and atlases are available via the book trade, although they may have to be special ordered from distributors like MapLink, who can also supply them directly to the consumer (see the Appendix for the address).

Getting There

Apart from cruise ships, almost all of which stop somewhere in Italy, there are ferry services to and from Greece, the French Riviera, Corsica, Barcelona, Tunis, and Malta. Italy, occupying a space in the center of the Mediterranean, has always been an important junction for travelers. The main international airports are at Milan, Rome, and Palermo, but it's difficult to find bargain fares in and out of the country. Trains are reliable and moderately priced, but also look into the possibility of the many inter-city buses, which are often cheaper and more convenient. They usually have room in the bottom compartment for a bike.

Although the stimulating landscape and culture make for an entertaining ride, cycling in Italy can be quite difficult except along the coasts. The terrain is mountainous: the Appennini range runs centrally 1200 km down the country from Liguria to Calabria, and the mighty Alps cover the northern part of the country. So though there are numerous routes into the country from France, Switzerland, Austria, and Croatia, traveling around the Riviera or the Adriatic helps the cyclist avoid the beautiful but strenuous mountain passes. But feel free to exit and reenter the tour whenever you feel strong and want to climb into the country's interior.

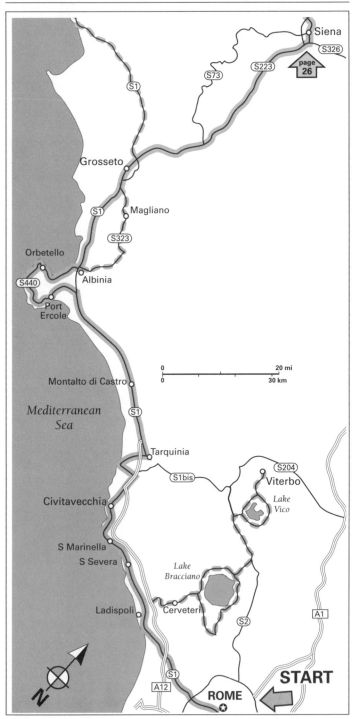

From Rome to the French Border

Total distance: 830 km (520 miles)
Terrain: mountainous
Duration: 6–14 days
Rating: moderate/difficult

I have broken the trip into sections. But don't think they are meant to be single-day trips, unless you're fit for the Giro d'Italia. Instead, each of these sections, being in the vicinity of 200–300 km, is a tour to be covered in several days. It's just that the beginning and end points of each stage are clearly recognizable destinations where you will want to stay some time and where you will find transportation in.

Section 1: From Rome to Siena

Distance: 276 km (172 miles)
Terrain: mountainous
Duration: 2–4 days
Rating: moderate

With so much to see in Rome—the Vatican Museum, the churches, the piazzas, the Forum and Colosseum, to name a few—it's possible to spend days sightseeing. However, it is not an ideal city for cycling because many of the older streets are cobblestone, Rome's drivers are notoriously incautious, and thieves proliferate in tourist areas.

Accommodations

You can find camping and various categories of hotels along the coast on SS1(SS stands for strada statale, or state route, but in this book, as in many maps, we'll use just one S—S1 for this route) and in Siena; medium-priced hotels ($40–$75) inland. Good places to stop are Santa Marinella, Civitavecchia, Tarquinia, Orbetello, and Grosseto.

1.1 *Rome to Tarquinia*

Distance: 88 km (55 miles)

1. Follow the signs to Livorno (Leghorn in English)and Pisa on the S1, and take the Via Aurelia, which starts just south of St. Peter's.

2. You face about 15 km of urban area until you go under the expressway, then 4 km later you pass an exit to Malagrotta. The ride is almost flat, and the multi-lane road carries a hefty share of traffic.

3. After a few more kilometers on this road, the traffic thins out as the road becomes one wide lane each way. You will see signs for a couple of castles on your right and a road that will take you to the beach town of Focene.

4. Continue north along the Via Aurelia next to the railroad, go over the Autostrada and pass several small communities until you arrive near the beach community of Ladispoli, 50 km from Rome.

5. Leave the main road in order to reach the sea area. From here all the way up the Aurelia you can find many camping areas, mostly on the west side of the road. The surrounding countryside is farmland or beach resort—the sea coast becomes more beautiful at this point, and the road begins to roll slightly.

6. Continue up the Via Aurelia about 4 km and turn right and slightly uphill toward Cerveteri.

7. As well as being an attractive modern town with a good view of the surrounding countryside, Cerveteri is an important Etruscan site with ruins and tombs from 2500 years ago.

8. From here you can investigate on your own the several scenic small roads to Lakes Bracciano and Vico. The roads that encircle these lakes, not at all flat, are especially pretty, and the old towns in this area are very nice to ride through.

9. For those who enjoy mountain riding, I can recommend the roads east of Viterbo, another important Etruscan city, which includes thermal springs.

10. Our tour returns to the Via Aurelia as we make our way hugging the coast to Civitavecchia.

11. Pass Santa Severa, an ancient Etruscan port, and Santa Marinella, both resorts with seaside castles.

12. Continuing, the ride is beautiful, with very slightly rolling hills next to the train track, all the way through Civitavecchia.

Civitavecchia

Civitavecchia is a large port city about 75 km from Rome. Young people gather here, strolling fashionably along the sea road for the evening passeggiata, and many cyclists either come or go through here since this is a major port for traveling to Sardinia and Corsica. The ferry run by the Italian railroad, FerroVia dello Stato, is located in a separate section of the port.

Continuation of Route

13. From the center of town, continue north along the coast past an industrial area. The S1 begins going inland, and you have to go uphill on the relatively quiet road.

14. At an intersection where there is some type of fort, you will see a sign for Lombardi. Take this small farm road, mildly rolling, for about 14 km until you see a sign for Tarquinia.

15. Cross over the Autostrada and climb slightly back to the Aurelia until you reach Tarquinia.

Tarquinia

Tarquinia, founded more than 3000 years ago, was once the home of the Tarquinian kings who ruled over Rome in pre-Republic times. It is a quaint town in a pretty setting, with an interesting museum containing Etruscan treasures. Although there is a campground close to the sea, finding a hotel room may be difficult, so ask at the tourist office.

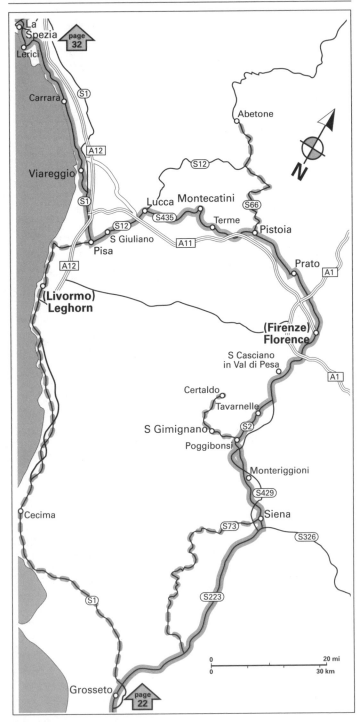

1.2 Tarquinia to Siena

Distance: 188 km (117 miles)

1. From Tarquinia, you can continue on the local road for a while, and then descend back to the Aurelia.

2. The road widens but becomes busier and noisier at this point.

3. Another 14 km on a hilly road brings us to Montalto di Castro. The castle with its imposing tower is 1000 years old, and it too has Etruscan tombs nearby.

Detour to Orbetello and Albinia

About 10 km from Montalto di Castro, there's a sign for Pescia Romana where you can turn right on the 9 km long Tombolo di Feniglia and toward the small town of Orbetello. You can either go into the city or you can continue toward the Tombolo di Giannella and follow the signs for Albinia. The roads here are flat and smooth, and you can return to the Aurelia for the continuation.

Continuation of Route

4. Follow the Via Aurelia for about 33 km to Grosseto. This part of the road is is busy, noisy, and flat.

5. One way is to take the S323 through Magliano and on to Grosseto. Alternately, you can stay on the S1. This route is more scenic, but harder—bear with it for a while.

6. Take the local S1 through Grosseto and follow the signs for Siena. This part of the route is difficult because of the mountains, but it is gorgeous. If you do not want to bike up hills, you can take a bus or train, or you can continue up the Aurelia, which remains between flat and rolling, and we'll meet you again in Pisa.

7. I have chosen but one of the several ways to reach Siena. From Grosseto, take the S223 north through the hills of the town. The road is generally quiet, but it is not especially wide and has three tunnels, so use care.

8. After passing the third tunnel you get a great view of the valley below. The road is slightly lonely, with only its hills, trees, and streams.

9. The last 5 km, when you're tired, is the most difficult, but at least the traffic doesn't dramatically increase as you approach Siena.

Siena

Sienna is a beautiful town. When Prince Charles was decrying London's lost beauty, he chose Siena as an example of a handsome city that is also an important commercial center. It's an Italian gem, with the Piazza del Campo, the Palazzo Comunale, the San Domenico Church, and the charming streets, shops, and houses. Signs direct you to the tourist office, which has a list of accomodations.

Section 2. From Siena to Genoa

Distance: 378–383 km (236–240 miles)
Terrain: mountainous, followed by flats and
                 rolling coast
Duration: 3–6 days
Rating: strenuous

This second part of our tour takes us around the mountains of central Italy through Firenze (Florence), through a valley to the sea, and finally up the coast to Genoa.

Accommodations

There is a range of hotels and hostels in all towns along this route, especially in Florence, Montecatini, Pisa, Viareggio, La Spezia and Genoa. There are adequate camping facilities along the coast.

2.1 Siena to Florence

Distance: 70 km (44 miles) direct

1. The ride from Siena to Florence is one of the harder parts of the tour. Leaving Siena, ride to Piazza Camollia and begin following the signs for Firenze (Florence), but don't get on the Autostrada.

2. Your route is marked clearly at San Dalmazio for the
    S429 toward Monteriggioni and Poggibonsi. This part of
    the road is very hilly.

3. The more difficult stretch extends 11 km to
    Monteriggioni, a lovely Tuscan town with scenic farms
    and vineyards throughout.

4. Between Monteriggioni and Poggibonsi (13 km), the
    road is less hilly. Passing a couple of villages along the
    way, you will reach the large city of Poggibonsi.

Detour to San Gimignano

A wonderful side trip is to take the road marked for San
Gimignano, a distance of 11 km. The road is hilly, but not
overly difficult. You'll pass wineries where you can
purchase a bottle to go with your dinner. Beautiful San
Gimignano is up on a hill, so keep your energy for the last
climb.

If you enjoyed that excursion, then follow the signs for
Certaldo, another lovely town 13 km away.

Continuation of Route

5. From Poggibonsi, continue on the S2, which parallels
    the highway.

6. On a moderately hilly road, cycle past San Martino, San
    Filippo, and arrive at Tavarnelle, 18 km from Poggibonsi.

7. The next main town on the S2 is San Casciano in Val di
    Pesa, about 15 km from Florence.

8. The road becomes markedly less hilly as you go under
    the Autostrade and start hitting the suburbs of the large
    urban area of Florence.

Florence and Surroundings

Make sure to get a guided tour of the city, or at a minimum
buy a guide book and use it to explore the city, including
surrounding villas, so you can catch at least some of the
numerous highlights of Florence.

One short side trip from Florence leads to the ancient
city of Fiesole on a 300 m high hill just north of the city. A
tough but rewarding climb, Fiesole is a uniquely beautiful

city with a terrific view of Florence. Start at Piazza della
Libertà in Florence and follow the signs for Fiesole.

2.2 Florence to Viareggio

Distance: 116 km (72 miles)

1. After leaving Florence, take the local Via Pistoiese
    through Sesto Florentino to Prato.

2. Though basically a large industrial city, Prato has a
    pleasant town center where you can find tasty biscotti
    made with almonds.

3. Follow the flat and well-marked Via Pistoiese to Pistoia
    as you pass nurseries and farm areas.

4. Pistoia has an impressive but simple cathedral and a
    brightly colored della Robbia frieze on the Ospedale del
    Ceppo. The roads north of Pistoia are very
    mountainous, going up to Abetone (1400 m), best
    known as a ski resort.

5. From Pistoia follow the signs for Montecatini. Shortly
    after leaving the city, the road becomes a bit tight, and
    you'll encounter a fairly major mountain along the way.

6. Just before the city of Montecatini, there's a turnoff to
    Monsummano, but continue straight into Montecatini, a
    thermal area since the days of ancient Rome and a
    pleasant place to spend time.

7. When leaving Montecatini, continue on the main road
    parallel to the railway line toward Buggiano, and take
    the small road through Alberghi to Collodi.

8. This is a hilly area with small roads that are hard to ride,
    but Pinocchio fans will want to check out Collodi—this
    character's "home town," where stores are full of Carlo
    Lorenzini memorabilia.

9. Backtrack down the hill and continue on the main road
    to Lucca, 42 km from Pistoia. The city of the composer
    Puccini, Lucca looks as if it hasn't changed since the
    Middle Ages.

10. To leave Lucca, ride on the street that goes around the
    wall and follow the sign for the S12 to Pisa, 22 km away.

11. Initially the road is flat, but before you reach San Giuliano it becomes uphill before descending into Pisa.

Pisa

If you stay on the road by which you enter town, it will take you near the Leaning Tower, which Galileo used in his scientific research. Once a mighty power on the Arno river, Pisa today is a rather sleepy town but for that one famous attraction. Other than the main square—the Piazza del Duomo, also known as the Field of Miracles—and its fine 11th-century cathedral, Pisa has enough hotel accommodation to satisfy the curious tourists, but very little for those on a tight budget, although there is an unofficial youth hostel (Ostello per la Gioventu).

Continuation of Route

12. Leaving Pisa, turn right at Via Cammeo, and take it north on the S1. After about 15 km of flat road, you arrive at the Viareggio area.

Viareggio

This is not a town but a region—a 30 km long stretched-out seaside resort, and it has a crowded road that passes along the sea. The area is lively, though not particularly stunning. Accommodation tends to be easier to find along this stretch than it is in Pisa.

2.3 Viareggio to Genoa

Distance: 157 km (98 miles)

1. Follow the road along the beach, which continues until Carrara, where the road begins going inland to La Spezia.

2. Follow the S331 uphill until you get to scenic Lerici, about 200 m above the sea.

Lerici

The town caters to the wealthy and has a splendid view of the harbor below. An expensive elevator will take you

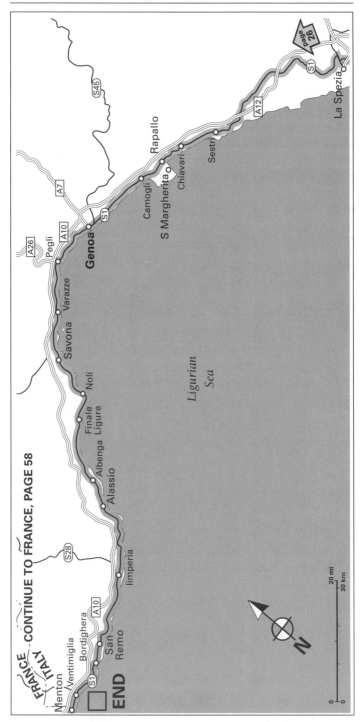

through the rock to the sea below, and you can go up to the 12th-century castle for an even more splendid view.

Continuation of Route

3. Shortly after you leave town you reach a tunnel that descends into the harbor town of La Spezia.

Riviera di Levante

The coast from here to Genoa is called the Riviera di Levante, and just near La Spezia is a popular walking area called Cinque Terre. Several writers and poets have stayed in this area and have written about its beauty. Perhaps you want to take a breather here, because the next part of the road is quite challenging, though scenic.

Continuation of Route

4. From La Spezia, climb up S1. In a little while the traffic thins out, and the road, surrounded by green hills, is a pleasant ride.

5. You pass several villages and rivers on the way as you labor over winding hills culminating 10 km outside Sestri at the 610 m high Bracco Pass.

6. After the tough climb to the pass, you descend easily back to the coast.

7. The remaining ride to Genoa is lovely, with hidden treasures along the way that are not in the guidebooks, so stay open to the possibilities that sponaneous sightseeing stops and side-trips afford.

8. The road is now moderately hilly, as it passes Cavi and Chiavari to arrive at the major resort of Rapallo, 15 km from Sestri.

Rapallo and Surroundings

This town has a seaside castle, Roman ruins, and a bridge used by Hannibal. From here you can ride a few km to Santa Margherita and Portofino, beautiful villages that have become chic places for Italians.

Continuation of Route

9. Continue on to Camogli and its narrow streets. Shortly
    thereafter is the noisy Genoa area; keep following the
    signs for the city center.

Genoa

Genoa, also written Genova, has an image problem as a
rough port city, but riding is especially fine on the wide Via
Garibaldi, and the historical center is one of the nicest in
Italy, with magnificent palazzos, churches, and art
museums. The city hosts fairs and cultural events, has its
own delicious cuisine, and is a good place to see modern
Italian life.

Section 3: From Genoa to the French Border

Distance: 170 km (106 miles)
Terrain: sea, coast
Duration: 2–3 days
Rating: moderate

This final section of the northern Italy tour continues along
the Riviera di Ponente to the French border. The ride isn't
flat, but it is breathtaking as you twist along the deep blue
sea and past the cliffs near San Remo and Bordighera. The
ups and downs on the road rarely exceed 100 m altitude.

   The only drawback to this part of the tour is the intense
amount of traffic, particularly in August. For the most part
the road is wide and not dangerous to cyclists, but it is noisy
with motorbikes and cars that also use this road. This area is
slightly more expensive than the rest of Italy, as seaside
resorts tend to be.

   Apart from the Autostrada, which you will see
traversing tunnel after tunnel, Viaduct after Viaduct, the
only road through the region is the ancient Via Aurelia. All
the other roads go inland, touching the rugged mountains.
But the route described here sticks to the coast and heads
west.

Accommodations

Plenty of hotels of all categories and camping are available,
but reservation for hotels is recommended in the high

season. As you enter a town, you will usually see a list of accommodations.

3.1 Genoa to Savona

Distance: 72 km (45 miles)

1. From the center of Genoa, follow the signs to Savona and Lungomare di Pegli in the direction of the airport.

2. Pass the large port area on a busy street and eventually reach a small harbor.

3. Continue on the S1, the Via Aurelia. You pass an unattractive beach area as you leave metropolitan Genoa, then, after about 16 km from the center, the road calms as the sea turns a beautiful blue.

4. Cogoleto, 25 km from central Genoa and our next town, is another pleasant seaside area, then the road takes a brief 1 km hill to reach Varazze, 5 km away, and passes elaborate centuries-old villas along the way.

5. You have a couple of winding hills before coming to Celle, but the road remains wide and the hills easy.

6. You start hitting the suburbs of the industrial city of Savona about 45 km from Genoa, passing through tunnels that cool you during the up-and-down ride.

3.2 Savona to Albenga

Distance: 45 km (28 miles)

1. From Savona, follow the signs for Ventimiglia, staying close to the port, and reach Spotorno after a gentle 10 km.

2. Follow the signs for Imperia, which takes you to the Antica Repubblica Marinara of Noli, which is definitely worth exploring since it has a well-preserved antique village near the hill fort.

3. Further on the S1 you come to Varigotti's clean beach, then Finale Liguria, Borgio Varezzi, Pietra Liguria, and Borghetto, all pleasant coastal communities with hotels, shops, and beaches.

4. The part of the Aurelia through Albenga is relatively flat.

5. At Albenga, stop and visit the cathedral and baptistry. Across the sea, you see the island of Gallinara

Camping areas abound and are well marked. I stayed at a comfortable place in Santa Anna sul Mare near Alassio.

3.3 Albenga to the French Border

Distance: 53 km (33 miles)

1. From Albenga, continue to Imperi,a which is 13 km away. You will have to go up the worst hill so far, about a 1.5 km climb, before reaching this interesting town.

2. A few km more takes you to San Lorenzo as you head to the famed resort of San Remo.

San Remo

Once an exclusive haunt for the rich, San Remo is now an Italian cultural center, which hosts annual pop music festivals and has many local clubs for young people. It's a lively, happy place.

Continuation of Route

3. Descend into Bordighera, one of the nicest communities along the way, then go toward Ventimiglia, which has Roman ruins and a medieval town.

4. Climb out of the city, go through a long tunnel, then climb again.

5. The short stretch between Ventimiglia and the French border—only a few km—is the most difficult part of this tour since the section near Sestri, and it culminates in a steep climb followed by a descend to the border.

6. There is a 2–3 km road to the top, where the Hanbury botanical garden, which has the most extensive selection of plants in Italy, overlooks the sea. Take a look at the French city of Menton, then wind downhill to the frontier station.

This brings you to the point where our tour of the French Mediterranean region, described in Chapter 4, starts.

Chapter 3
Italy South of Rome

This second Italian tour begins again in Rome, this time going south, as you travel past Naples (Napoli) to Salerno, a total distance of about 330 km. If possible, don't skip this part of the trip; cycling offers an intimate look at the backroads of southern Italy that taking a ferry or staying in one of the major cities doesn't provide.

A few different routes exist, but the most direct road is the antique S7, the Via Appia, which leads to this tour's final destination of Brindisi. The road is wide with a shoulder, but the traffic can be heavy. Another main road through this area, the Via Pontina, is same way. To avoid these drawbacks, we will follow a more scenic sea route which only adds about 35 km to our journey.

For a brief general discourse on the way the route is described, as well as what kind of situations to expect cycling in Italy and how to prepare for them, see the opening section of Chapter 2, *Italy North of Rome*. If you

choose to use the d'Agostini maps, get sheets 11, 12, 13, 14, 15, and16 for this tour.

Section 1. From Rome to Salerno

Distance: 330 km (206 miles)
Terrain: coastal road with some mountains
Duration: 2–4 days
Rating: moderate

Accommodations

There is no shortage of hotels and camping along the coast between Rome and Gaeta, with fewer accommodation options until the Naples area, where there are many hotels, and camping at Pompeii. Avoid rock-bottom hotels around Naples, because they are as nasty as they are cheap.

1.1 Rome to Terracina

Distance: 145 km (91 miles)

1. In Rome, begin your ride at the Colosseum and negotiate your way to the Pyramide area.

2. Follow either Via Ostensea or Via Christoforo Colombo: unfortunately, neither way is ideal since the first few km

are, like all of Rome's main streets, busy and poorly paved. Via Ostensea becomes Via Portuense, which is narrower but less trafficked than our other option, Via Christoforo Columbo, which becomes S8, Via del Mare. I prefer Via Poruense which, although longer and narrower, has less traffic.

3. On either road, follow the signs for Ostia Antica, passing a mixture of urban and farm area.

4. Turn onto the S296 and view the ancient area's extensive ruins.

5. Take a smaller road parallel to the S296 to arrive at the seaside town of Ostia Antica, where modern Romans vacation.

6. Turn left when you get to the sea.

7. When exiting Ostia Antica, continue southeast on the beach road. Public and private beaches line your route on this pleasant four-lane Via Severiana (S601).

8. Passing by the towns of Torvaianica, and 20 km later, Lavinio, your ride is flat and not heavily trafficked as you head toward the Anzio-Nettuno area. Particularly attractive is the thriving beach area around Nettuno.

9. From Nettuno, follow the signs to Latina and ride inland on a quiet, tree-lined road. Stay on this road for 8 km, then follow Lido di Latina and Foce Verde back to the coast. You are likely to encounter some headwind along the coast since the sea breeze often blows from the south during summer. Generally this breeze increases as the day goes on, so try to get your best riding in the morning.

10. Remain on the beach road or head south on the inland road; either route will take you around the cape.

11. Follow the signs to Terracina and you will hit the S148, a wide but busy road that merges into the S7, the Via Appia, at the 107 km marker.

12. Take the turnoff to Terracina and go through town. The camping areas near Terracina are superior to those in the preceding areas. Terracina is a large and gracious city dominated by a cliff.

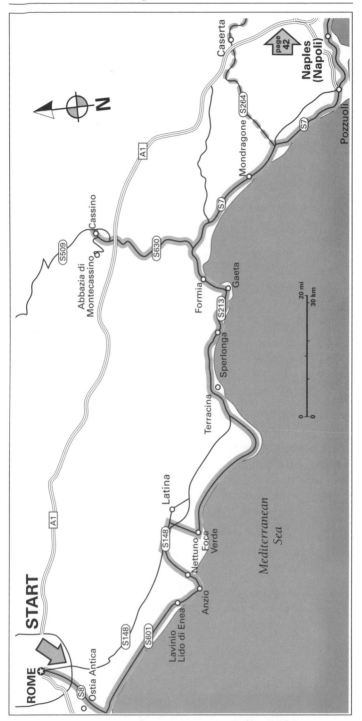

1.2 Terracina to Naples

Distance: 110 km (69 miles)

1. From the center of Terracina, descend to the sea, which is beautiful here, and follow the signs for Napoli (Naples), 125 km away. Traffic is light, but the road is a bit narrow in spots.

2. Continue flat to Sperlonga, a pleasant seaside community that sits partly on a cliff with a fortress by the sea. Up to this point the terrain has been flat, but now a couple of hills pop up along the way.

3. After the first climb and descent, you enter four tunnels: 250 m, 185 m, 590 m, and 200 m in length. Be careful here, and preferably use a headlight and rear reflector, especially in the three shorter tunnels, which are not illuminated.

4. This road, called the Via Flacca after you pass Sperlonga, is incredibly beautiful with some moderate hills.

5. Make the turn at the bottom of the peninsula, then enter into the large Gaeta-Formia urban area, which is neither strikingly beautiful nor terribly interesting. However, you may take a ferry to nearby islands from the port.

6. Just after Formia there's a turnoff for the S630 to Cassino, 40 km away. The road to Cassino is busy but wide, with a relatively easy hilly area coming after San Georgio.

7. From near Cassino you can see the famous monastery of St. Benedict atop the hill, with a hairpin road leading to the top.

8. Returning to the coastal road, ignore the signs to Naples at several turnoffs. Instead, stay to your right on the scenic coastal road, as the inland road is a rather busy four-lane road.

9. After Formia, ride through Santa Croce and Minturna where you pass a Roman theatre. The road is quite busy here, but there is a marked shoulder.

10. Bypass the Autostrade and remain on the S7.

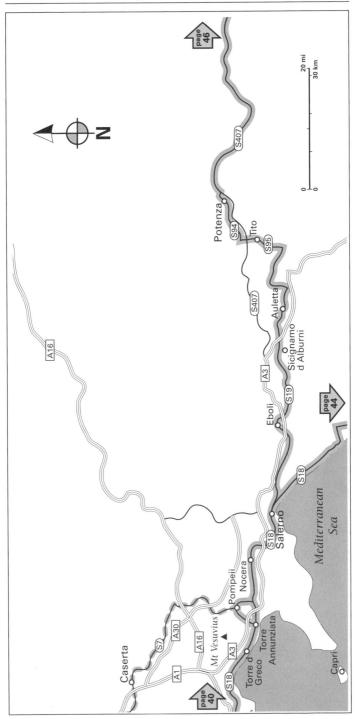

11. Travel 18 km to Mondragone and another 13 km to Castel Volturno, then take the unmarked local road to Pozzuoli. There aren't many road signs here, but it's clear which is the main road, and everyone is willing to direct you.

Pozzuoli

As this is one of the nicest towns in the Naples region, you may consider staying here. Try the local specialty of Buffalo mozzarella cheese or sample some of the many other fine pastries and delicatessen delights. As described below under *Naples*, you may consider getting on a train in Pozzuoli and avoid many of the hazards—and some of its undeniable fascination.

Continuation of Route

12. Continue along the same road, and near Ischitella take the S7 (Via Domitiana) to Naples.

13. Five km out of Pozzuoli you have your first climb, which affords a splendid view of the city and gulf below.

14. In the area known as the Campi Flegrei or Phlegrean Fields, there's a steep 3 km climb followed by a descent. The local road will take you into Bagnoli, another fascinating old town, and from there it's best to follow the main road to Napoli Centro, the city center.

Naples and Surroundings

The Naples (Napoli in Italian) region is a large, overpopulated urban area extending from Pozzuoli to Salerno. The picturesque location, mild climate, and archeological remains make this an interesting city to visit. Unfortunately, Naples has fallen on hard times in recent decades. Much of the road is practically rubble and more uncomfortable to ride than a dirt road. The traffic can at best be described as chaotic and at worst it is downright dangerous. With its extremes of wealth and poverty, beauty and ugliness, Naples has a very different feel than the rest of Italy.

If you would like to avoid the particular dangers of Naples, either go to the train station at Pozzuoli and take the train to Salerno, or avoid the area altogether by riding

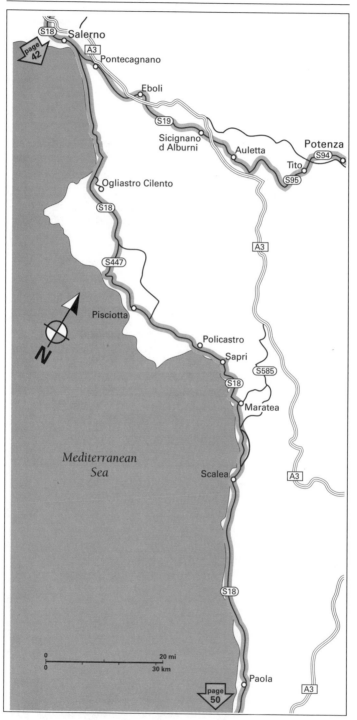

through Caserta. But if you decide to ride through Naples, you won't regret the experience as long as you remain alert. The Napolitani are outgoing, kind, friendly, and fun, and riding through here is invigorating. If you like, you can take a ferry to the famous islands of Ischia and Capri from Pozzuoli, Sorrento, or Naples.

You probably will need to stay at a hotel in the Spaccanapoli district, or Greater Naples, to explore the sights, since the area lacks campgrounds, the only ones being at Pompeii. There's much to see here, but don't let down your guard against thieves.

1.3 Naples to Salerno

Distance: 75 km (47 miles)

1. From Naples, follow the coastal road out of the city, with Mount Vesuvius looming in the distance.

2. Continue on the same road and follow the signs for Pompeii, as you wind around the narrow, hilly streets.

3. Stay alert to traffic from behind, looking back or using your rearview mirror, if you have one, and use your hands to signal rather than relying on the traffic lights.

4. Look for signs leading to Vesuvio (Vesuvius) and Ercolano (Herculaneum).

Vesuvius and Herculaneum

The volcano's last eruption was as recent as WWII, and it is expected to boil over again by the end of the century. The ancient city of Herculaneum, snuffed out by the volcano in 79 AD, has left many fascinating ruins. The train station in this otherwise harsh-looking city will keep your bicycle while you tour the area on foot. I've never taken the road to the top of Vesuvius, but those who have say it's beautiful but cold.

Continuation of Route

5. Continue following the signs to Pompeii. Keep in mind that all the cities in this area overlap so that it's difficult to tell exactly where you are unless you ask someone.

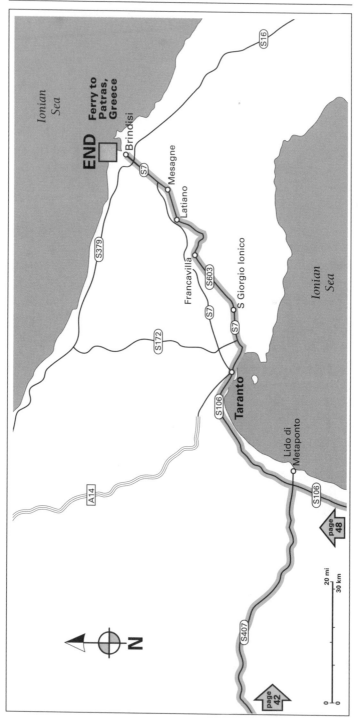

6. Torre Annunziata, a few km before Pompeii, has a reputation as a rough town, so you may not want to stop here.

7. Keep traveling on an unnervingly rough road to Pompeii. The distance is only about 45 km but feels longer since you have to go slowly.

Pompeii

As you enter Pompeii, you see two campgrounds, one of which allowed me to keep my bike in a safe room as I explored the ancient city. Pompeii is safe in comparison to many of the other cities in this region and offers a large number of remarkable sights for the visitor. Allow yourself several hours to visit the fascinating ruins.

Continuation of Route

8. When leaving Pompeii, continue on the road to Salerno, going through Scafati, Angri, Pagani, Nocera, and Cava. Road signs are missing, and the streets are hilly, narrow, and uneven.

9. The worst hill is about a 4 km climb up to Ogliara just before Salerno. As you descend, you are treated to a wonderful view of the sea and the Gulf of Salerno.

Vesuvius looming over the remains of one of its historic victims: Pompeii.

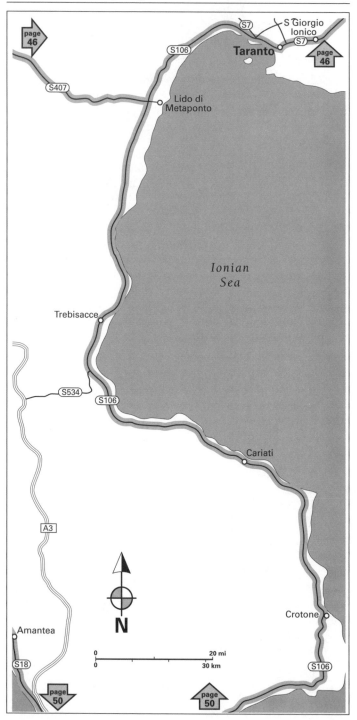

Section 2. From Salerno to Brindisi and Sicily

This section of the tour leads to our destination, Brindisi, where we can take a ferry to Greece. You cannot avoid mountains on this route unless you take the train, but there are two options, referred to as Routes A and B below: the shorter Route A traverses the Apennine mountains through Potenza, and Route B continues down the coast to Sicily and then continues to the east coast.

Route A. The Potenza Route

Distance: 260 km (162 miles)
Terrain: mountainous
Duration: 2–4 days
Rating: strenuous

Accommodations

Not plentiful until you reach the east coast. The larger towns have at least a two- or three-star hotel. All the villages we pass are peaceful, and the habitants are hospitable—most people will let you camp on their property for the night.

1. Leave Salerno by following the signs for Reggio C. and Pontecagnano on the S18 along the coast.

2. Go through Pontecagnano on a rolling road for about 17 km to reach Battipaglia, a large tomato canning center that exports around the world.

3. Go through the center of town to a large roundabout and follow the signs for Eboli, another 7 km.

4. Steadily going uphill, you pass under the Autostrada to reach Eboli.

5. After leaving Eboli, cross over the Autostrada, and follow the signs for S19 to Cosenza. After leaving Eboli, the road becomes more difficult.

6. You face a fairly serious 5 km climb into Serre, which is about 200 m in altitude.

7. Ride through the town on the S19, a nice country road lined with grape, olive, and fig trees toward Scorzo.

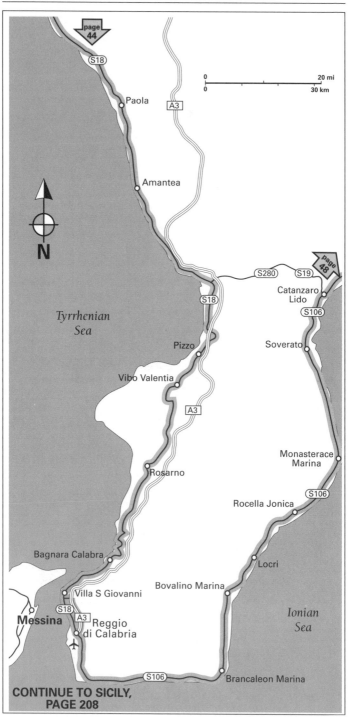

page 44

S18

Paola

A3

Amantea

0   20 mi
0   30 km

page 48

S280   S19

Catanzaro
Lido

S106

S18

*Tyrrhenian
Sea*

Pizzo

Soverato

Vibo Valentia

A3

Monasterace
Marina

Rosarno

S106

Rocella Jonica

Bagnara Calabra

Locri

Bovalino Marina

Villa S Giovanni

*Ionian
Sea*

S18   A3

Messina

Reggio
di Calabria

S106

Brancaleon Marina

**CONTINUE TO SICILY,
PAGE 208**

8. After Scorzo, you descend a 15% grade to tiny Zuppino, then you continue straight to Auletta on the S19.

9. Shift into low gear to climb the steep 6 km to Auletta; then climb again another 6 km to the main road, the S19 ter.—the first 4 km are steep and hard.

10. Next, turn left, following the direction for Potenza.

11. Continue about 6 km until you see a sign pointing right for Potenza on the S94. The remaining road to Potenza is quite hilly at first but tapers off gradually into a pleasant ride.

12. You pass Tito, an industrial area, then enter the city center.

13. To reach the coast, take the S407. Unlike the stretch west of Potenza, this road is in good condition and safe, except for five short unlit tunnels and four long lit tunnels—550 m, 600 m, 800 m, and 630 m long. Be careful: use a light and rear reflector, stay to the right, and don't let the noise of cars upset you.

14. The S407 runs through a valley surrounded by picturesque mountaintop villages. It's a wonderful road for fast riding: you feel like you're constantly going downhill.

15. At the end you pass under the S106 and have the option of heading toward Taranto or proceeding straight to Metaponto. There are two campgrounds here: the first just after you enter from the S407 and the other about 10 km from Taranto.

16. The 48 km to Taranto are mostly flat. Go to the center of Taranto, an industrial and military hub. Then follow the signs for San Giorgio Ionico (13 km) and Lecce. Don't follow the signs for Brindisi here, because they lead to the main road, which is noisy and unpleasant compared to the quiet farm roads we will be following. The traffic on the road to San Giorgio Ionico gets lighter as you leave Taranto.

17. Turn left at the sign for Brindisi and arrive at Carosino.

18. Follow the signs for Francavilla on S603. After the 9 km mark, turn right at the sign for Oria.

19. Travel the 12 km to Oria and view the countryside around you from the town's castle.

20. To reach Brindisi, follow the signs for Latino and continue through the town of Mesagne. Take the S7 (Via Appia) to Brindisi. A column marks the end of this ancient road.

21. Enter the town, and at the roundabout, follow the signs for the port. You will see several places to buy ferry tickets for destinations such as Egypt, Turkey, and Corfu. For our tour of Greece (Chapter 6), we will take the ferry to Patras, a journey of about 18 hours.

Route B. The Coastal Road

Distance:	429 km (268 miles)
Terrain:	mountainous and coastal
Duration:	4–6 days
Rating:	strenuous in parts

This alternative route travels toward Sicily by means of the coastal road from Salerno, then turns east and thus avoids crossing the mountains, without necessarily making this an easy route, because there are still plenty of ups and downs.

Accommodations

Plan your ride to end at a town, as there is nothing in between. Most towns have at least one mid-range hotel. There are several campgrounds.

1. From Salerno, instead of going inland to Battipaglia, continue along the road near the sea until you reach the ruins near Spinazzo.

2. Turn inland and follow the signs for Ogliastro. The road is very hilly, so be prepared for some difficult climbs.

3. Stay on the S18, then cycle another 3 km to Prignano.

4. The next 15 km are easy and scenic as you follow the signs for Vallo, but 3 km out of the town you face another hard climb.

5. The road then descends into Laurito, from which point it's hilly all the way to Torre Orsaia.

6. From here it's down hill to the coastal village of Policastro. Continue along the sea to Sapri, where you can at least take courage in knowing that the hardest part of this tour is now behind you, but you still have many miles, if not quite as much climbing, ahead of you.

7. You face a serious 3 km climb into Maratea before descending again to the coast at Scalea.

8. After 5 km, join the main road and continue on to Cirella.

9. Head to Diamante on the local road, then rejoin the S18 which leads inland.

10. Continue through Amantea, go through an unlit tunnel, and stay on the main road to Pizzo.

11. After Pizzo, follow the signs for Vibo Valentia. This area has a few camping areas, staggered about 20–30 km apart.

12. Take the road to Vibo Valentia for about 7 km, then ascend the pretty road to Mileto and Rosarno.

13. Twist back down to the coast at Gioia, where there's a local road to Palmi.

14. Return to the S18 and continue south, climbing for about 7 km then descending to Bagnara Calabra.

15. Passing Scilla, go around the coast to Villa San Giovanni.

Connection with Sicily

It's possible from here to take the ferry (traghetto) across the Strait of Messina to Sicily. Follow the signs for "Traghetto" to get to the port. See Chapter 16 for a description of the Sicily tour.

Continuation of Route

16. From the port at Villa San Giovanni (or from the ferry back from Sicily), head to the Adriatic Coast by following the blue signs for Reggio di Calabria and continue through the town. On a clear day you can look back across the strait and see the top of Mt. Etna in the middle of Sicily.

17. Stay on the S106 which continues along the sandy beaches of the Ionian Sea into Bovalino Marina. The road curves and climbs, but the sights are truly splendid in this part of Italy.

18. At Catanzaro Lido, you encounter more traffic as you head further inland.

19. Continue on this wide road along the coast past Crotone, and later you reach Lido di Metaponto. The rest of the road to Brindisi is described for Route A.

Chapter 4
France

Anyone who loves cycling will enjoy the beautiful country roads of France. There's nothing like getting up early in the morning and going for an exhilarating ride on narrow farm roads and stopping for coffee and chocolate croissants at an outdoor café in a rustic village.

France is easily accessible by land, sea, or air, so shop around for bargain fares. The most important ingredient for a successful French bike trip is a good map that details the small farm roads, for once you're on any of them, riding is a joy. I recommend you locally buy the appropriate Michelin yellow-cover regional series maps at scale 1:200,000 (you'll need sheets 240 and 245), which are probably the most detailed maps you'll ever find at this scale.

In France, the blue road signs point toward the Autoroute, whereas the green signs usually refer to the Route National (N). Generally, you should follow the white signs for the local roads, but occasionally you will need to take the busier N routes at least part of the way. All roads are well marked, but despite all the road signs, asking directions is usually necessary.

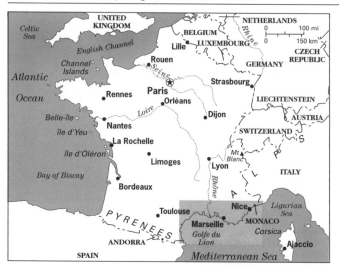

France is about the most expensive country of any described in this book, but budget travelers can also locate plenty of places to eat and sleep. Campsites and hostels are about the same price as in the rest of Europe, and if you prepare your own meals, you can spend as little as $20 a day.

From the Italian Border to the Spanish Border

Total distance: 650 km (406 miles)
Terrain: coast and country
Duration: 5–10 days
Rating: moderate to difficult

I have incorporated the wonderful variety of French countryside into this route. We will head west around the Riviera toward Spain, then move inland through rural roads, returning to the coast for the final segment. Parts of the tour are difficult, but never stressful. The two sections of the tour are joined midway by the beautiful town of Aix-en–Provence. The route starts where the tour of northern Italy ends, at Menton on the Italian border.

Section 1. From Menton to Aix-en-Provence

Distance:	255 km (160 miles)
Terrain:	a mixture of coast and farmland
Duration:	2–5 days
Rating:	difficult

Accommodations

There are plenty of hotels of all categories, especially upscale, and many hostels and campgrounds along the sea. Inland, hotels and hostels can be found in the larger towns.

1.1 Monaco to St. Raphael

Distance: 162 km (101 miles)

1. Beginning near the Italian border at Menton, cycle west along the harbor.

2. Follow the signs for the D52 to Monaco, which is about 20 km from the border. Climb a hill, and then cycle the coast to the famous principality of Monaco and the city of Monte Carlo.

Monte Carlo

There's no need to advise you about not gambling since the casino will not let you near the door in your biking outfit. Bike around and spend some time enjoying the fancy shops, the port with its splendid yachts, and the town's festive atmosphere.

Continuation of Route

3. Descending to the harbor, follow the signs for Nice and Basse Corniche and go up a hill to Villefranche-sur-Mer. It's a moderate climb with a lot of traffic, but is preferable to the N7 coastal route and the inland D2564 until you reach Nice after about 15 km.

Nice

Nice is the major center of the French Riviera, or Côte d'Azur, as it is called in French, with ferry service to other coastal cities as well as to the island of Corsica (which we

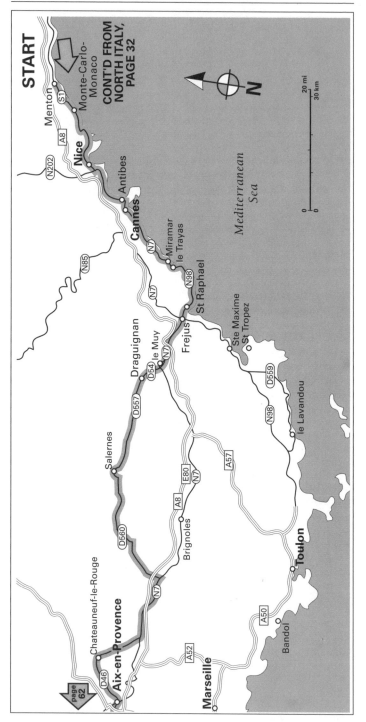

START

Menton

Monte-Carlo-
Monaco

CONT'D FROM
NORTH ITALY,
PAGE 32

S1

A8

N202

Nice

Antibes

Cannes

N7

Miramar
le Trayas

N85

N7

N98

St Raphael

Draguignan

le Muy

Frejus

Ste Maxime
St Tropez

D54

D557

N7

D559

Salernes

N98

le Lavandou

A57

D560

E80
N7

A8

Brignoles

Chateauneuf-le-Rouge

N7

Toulon

Aix-en-Provence

A50

D46

A52

Bandol

page
62

Marseille

*Mediterranean
Sea*

N

20 mi
30 km

0
0

cover in Chapter 15). Nice is a fun and lively place, offering the tourist para-sailing, water skiing, swimming and sunbathing. Those interested in sea life should visit the Oceanographic Museum, while those more interested in people-watching can just hang out along the boardwalk.

Continuation of Route

4. Continue along the eight lane Promenade des Anglais past the airport on the N98 in the direction of Cannes and Antibes (23 km from Nice). This section of the road, unlike the east side of Nice, is a completely flat beach area.

5. Just after the resort of Cagnes, the road becomes a pleasant local drive.

6. Keep following the signs for Antibes on the N98. About 11 km from Nice you reach Villeneuve, then after ascending one short hill you arrive at Antibes.

7. When you're ready to leave Antibes, return to the N7 and follow the signs to Cannes and Juan-les-Pins.

8. The 9 km stretch to Cannes is heavily trafficked but flat. Enjoy the essence of life on the Cote d'Azur here in Cannes or head up to Grasse, source of most of the world's perfume and surrounded by lovely hills of lavender. However, the nicest part of the French coast still awaits you between Cannes and St. Raphael along the N98 coastal road.

9. Go through the city of Napoule past the Hotel Royal Casino to Theoule, where the road becomes quieter but hillier. The port of Theoule has a large castle.

10. Climb out of Theoule for 2 km to look over the wide expanse of blue bay and see the islands of Ste. Marguerite and St. Honorat.

11. Wind down the road and continue to Le Trayas, where you must tackle one of the hardest, but most gorgeous, climbs so far.

12. After Le Trayas, the road is up and down along the scenic brown cliffs. This area is less crowded in contrast to the heavy traffic around the flats between Nice and Antibes.

13. Pass through the village of Antheor and go around the bay as you continue to the harbor town of Agay, which has several campgrounds near it.

14. Continue to St. Raphael, a large harbor and beach community about 70 km from Nice.

1.2 St. Raphael to Aix-en-Provence

Distance: 77 km (48 miles)

1. To leave St. Raphael, take the N7 west and follow the signs for Draguignan-en-Provence past the ruins of a Roman amphitheater. The first few km on the busy national road are relatively peaceful, with moderate traffic on a wide, tree-lined road.

2. There are several campgrounds along the way to Le Muy (10 km), which has an interesting church and bell tower. Passing several roundabouts, you follow the signs to the town center of Le Muy.

3. When leaving Le Muy, instead of taking the busy N555 to Draguignan, follow the signs for the D54 to La Motte. Take this quiet road to the village of La Motte.

4. Follow the white sign to Draguignan from town and turn on the D59. Draguignan is a pleasant old city.

5. Follow the signs for the D557, and leave Draguignan by climbing a winding hill with a good view of the city below.

6. After a 4 km climb, the road splits; take the fork leading to Salarnes, 18 km away.

7. Climb a bit more on the D557 until you come to a roundabout at the top, then continue following the signs for Salarnes. The rest of the way is all rolling hills on a narrow, quiet road.

8. Passing the medieval village of Flayosc, which has a campground, take the old farm road along this scenic route.

9. After the turnoff for the D10, arrive at an intersection where the D557 forks right—but continue straight here.

10. Stop at Salarnes, then head west on the same road in the direction of Marseille and Barjols. The peaceful road is surrounded by greenery, stone buildings, a few villages, and, if you're there in the summer, fields of sunflowers.

11. Descend into Barjols and stay on the D560. The bottom of the hill brings you to the base of another winding hill, so continue up the road.

12. Pass the small village of Brue-Auriac, which has a quaint courtyard in front of an old church.

13. As you approach St. Maximin the road becomes busier, but it has a shoulder for bicycles.

14. Go to the center of St. Maximin and make a right turn onto the unmarked main road, which is actually N7 again.

15. Follow the green signs toward Trets and Aix-en-Provence. Trets, which is just off the N7, is the central city for this wine-growing region.

16. With a mountain range to your right, you can continue on the N7 into Aix-en-Provence, or you can take several smaller roads all leading to this large town. I suggest leaving the N7 at Chateauneuf-le-Rouge and turning north for about a km through vineyards until you hit the D46 for Antenne.

17. Wind around the D17 through Le Tholonet and continue on the many one–way streets to the center of Aix-en-Provence.

Aix-en-Provence

Known as the city of Cezanne, this large city was founded in Roman times and hosts one of the most important music festivals in France. Aix's famous main street, the Cours Mirabeau, is exciting to bike or walk along.

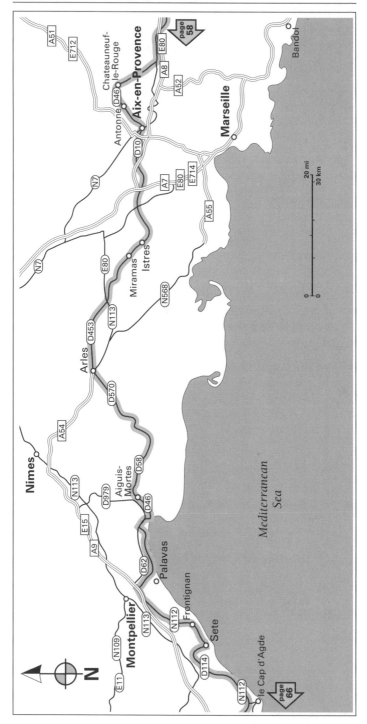

Section 2. From Aix-en-Provence to the Spanish Border

Distance: 395 km (246 miles)
Terrain: flat or mild hilly
Duration: 4–6 days
Rating: moderate

Accommodations

Except for a stretch between Arles and Aiques Mortes, you are never far from camping or hotels. The large cities have youth hostels. Good places to stop include Miramas, Arles, the coastal towns between Aiguis Mortes and Carnon, Montpellier, Sète, Bèziers, Narbonne, and Argelès.

2.1 Aix-en-Provence to Montpellier

Distance: 175 km (109 miles)

The second phase of our tour continues west through the region of Provence before heading south to Spain. Much of this route is flat.

1. To leave Aix, go in the direction of Berre on the D10 and stay on this easy road to the quaint town of La-Fare-les-Oliviers.

2. Go over the Autoroute to where the D10 becomes a small country road.

3. Follow the signs for St. Chamas, 12 km from La Fare, and pass an old chateau at Les Guigues.

4. Continue on the D10 to Miramas, 31 km from Aix.

5. The D10 remains quiet and flat for another 6 km. Pass a large railway yard on your left and a military barracks on your right, and follow the signs for Arles and St. Martin.

6. Go north on the D5 and turn onto the N113 for about 6 km.

7. Take the first turnoff for St. Martin and go into the city.

8. Instead of continuing on the N113, take the D453 through Raphele-les-Arles and Balarin to arrive at Arles.

This beautiful city, home of Vincent Van Gogh, has been a thriving center for the arts for the last decade. Enjoy walking around the streets of the town and touring the surrounding countryside.

9. From Arles, continue southwest to Aiguis Mortes by following the signs for St. Giles on the D570 and D572.

10. About 7 km from Arles, turn at the sign for Albaron (there's a campground at the turnoff). We're now on the D37, another quiet country road.

11. When you see the turnoff for Aigues Mortes, make a right and you'll be on the D38c. You then cross over the Petit Rhone. This area is like Louisiana or the coastal area of Scotland; there's a restaurant or two and some camping, but not much other than the flat, empty road.

12. After 12 km in that weedy area, you start hitting vineyards and farms.

13. Follow the signs for Aiguis Mortes and La Grande Motte, and turn left on the D46. Aiguis Mortes has nice roads for cycling—flat, smooth, and reasonably quiet.

14. Follow the D62 to La Grande Motte (9 km), a lively place with pyramid-shaped hotels, glitzy shops, new apartment buildings, exciting boardwalks, and harbors of sleek boats. It and the surrounding towns are crowded in the summer, while at other times of the year you can have the whole road to yourself.

15. Don't get back on the D62 as you leave La Grande Motte. Instead, stay along the beach and take the local road to Carnon, about 10 km away. The main highway (D62), with two tight lanes full of traffic each way, is really a nightmare for cyclists.

16. Around Carnon you will find a bike path that will take you to the local roads.

17. From Carnon to Montpellier, the area has so many roads that you may become confused if you don't carry a detailed map or stay close to the main road. The main road itself is pretty heavily trafficked, so it will be better to take the unmarked side roads that parallel the D986 to Montpellier. The historic city of Nostradamus,

Montpellier is a university town with many young people.

2.2 Montpellier to the Spanish Border

Distance: 220 km (137 miles)

1. When you're ready to leave Montpellier, continue west on the N112 from the center of town. This is not a terrific road for cycling, but it does have a nice wide shoulder.

2. When you reach Frontignan, cut across the D129 and follow the signs to Sète, an historic canal town with a network of bridges connecting two islands. The road levels as you approach the sea.

3. From Sète, continue around la Corniche on the D114 until it leads back into the N112.

4. The N112 is a straight beach road, with a field of reeds on your right side. It does have traffic but is sufficiently wide.

5. Continue to Agde, 18 km from Sète, a picturesque city with a canal and colorful boats.

6. Cross the railroad tracks and the canal and follow the signs in the center of Agde for the D13 to Bessan (8 km), a surprisingly large town.

7. From here continue following the signs for Bèziers, 17 km away on the D28.

8. After 8 km, at Coussergues, continue on the D28 under the Autoroute and follow the signs for Bèziers. Dominated by a castle on a hill,this is not a large town and is a good place to relax among the tree-lined streets. Take the opportunity to sample some of the local wines, since you are in the region's central wine-growing area.

9. When leaving Bèziers, go downhill on the N9 to a turnoff for the D14. This area, slightly rolling at first and then entirely flat, is overflowing with grapes. If you are adventurous, there are numerous other small unpaved roads through the vineyards that ultimately reconnect; otherwise, stay on the D14.

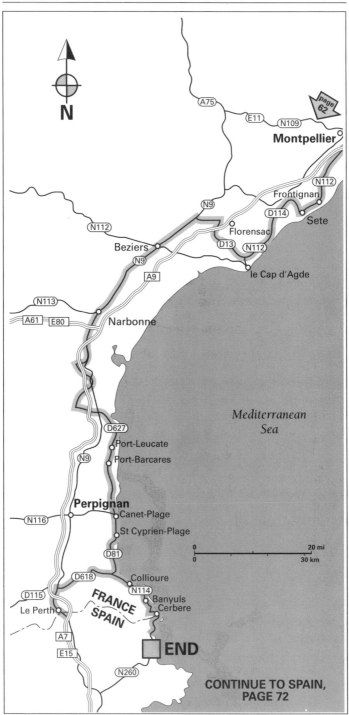

CONTINUE TO SPAIN, PAGE 72

10. Continue straight at Lespignan, about 14 km from Beziers, to Fleury, 7 km.

11. Go underneath the expressway and cross over the small river l'Aude. Wind through the narrow streets of Fleury and turn left on the D1118 for 2 km to Salles, with camping nearby.

12. At the Salles roundabout, follow the signs for Vinassian. On the way, you will pass Chateau Celeyran as well the family home of Toulouse-Lautrec.

13. From Vinassian, continue on the D31 and follow the signs for Narbonne. From here, it's a pleasant ride to the Spanish border.

14. Leave Narbonne via the N9 south.

15. About 1 km beyond the intersection to the Autoroute you'll see a shrine on your right and a sign for the D105 to Bages, 4 km. Turn left and go underneath the Autoroute on this curvy, narrow, and quiet country lane.

16. Passing more vineyards, visit Bages and the next town, Peyriac (6 km) with camping.

17. From Peyriac, continue straight on the D105 until you come to the N9 again, and turn left.

18. Continue until you reach the intersection marked D627.

19. Turn left, west, to Port-Leucate, a dry flat area. From now on the only thing to contradict the flatness of the road is an overpass or two as you pass a strip of land between the sea and the bay. There's a small stretch of unpleasant road south of Le Lydia up to Le Barcarès where the road is four lanes with heavy traffic.

20. After Le Barcarès, 14 km from Port-Leucate, the coastal road passes Torreiles (3 km), St. Marie Plage (5 km), and Canet Plage (3 km), all seaside resorts.

21. There is no need to go to the main part of Canet, so continue on the local road near the beach, then go to the D81a toward St. Cyprien-Plage.

22. Stay on the flat coastal road and follow the signs for the Plage, not for St. Cyprien itself.

23. At St. Cyprien-Plage, continue through the roundabouts to the D81. The area has camping and some isolated spots for swimming.

24. Shortly, you'll reach Argelès, a summer apartment community that mushroomed in the 1980s, which is a pleasant area crowded with cyclists and pedestrians.

25. From here, continue south on D81 through several roundabouts and turn onto the D114, which soon becomes the N114. Take this road for a couple of km to Collioure (6 km from Argelès).

26. At Collioure, go inland and take the N9 north of Perpignan, where the road gets slightly hilly.

27. The N9 becomes narrow near the Spanish border, and at Le Perthus, it descends into town, where there are stores and money changers.

Coastal Alternate Route

1. If, instead of taking the inland route along the N9, you stay on the coast and continue along the D86 at the roundabout to Port Vendres, you get to the N114 at Port Vendres.

2. From here, it's another 6 km to Banyuls, where there is a serious hill that yields a panoramic view of the sea and Port Vendres. This nice asphalted road becomes moderately hilly and narrow, but there's ample room for your bicycle.

3. After Banyuls, it's a 8 km winding and hilly road to Cerbère, and from there it's another hard 3 km climb to the border station.

This is where our tour of Spain picks up the route—see Chapter 5.

Chapter 5

Spain

Flamenco, bull fights, Joan Miro, sangria, beaches, barren mountains—Spain has it all, including great bicycle touring. It does not have as many backroads as France because the countryside is less populated, so we must use main roads more often than not. Spain's road surface, once a point of criticism by cyclists, has improved immensely during the last decade. Most of the area we are traveling to is beautiful, the people very friendly and welcoming.

Bicycle Touring in Spain

Spain is a moderately expensive country for bicycle touring. It is cheaper than France and England and probably about the same price as the United States. Pitching your tent in a campground will usually cost under $10. You can fill your day's supply of food and water at the grocery store for about the same price. Southern Spain gets very hot during July and August, so try to avoid riding there during that time.

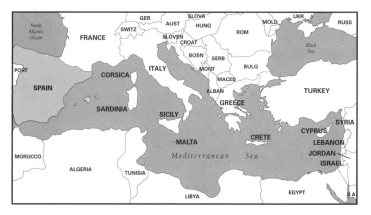

Spain's festivals, especially in the south, are colorful and a lot of fun. Many towns have weekend festivals during summer, and several cities are renowned for their elaborate Holy Week and saint day celebrations. The Spanish tourist offices can give you a list of these. Bullfights occur in the large cities from March to mid-October on Sunday afternoon and cost about $30. Cycling is another national sport, and many local cyclists will join you on the road, especially on Sunday. Strike up a conversation with them, and they will help you discover little-known shrines and other spots not listed in the guidebooks.

Our tour travels along the Spanish east coast from France to the tip of Spain directly across from North Africa. It's a popular route, followed by many other cyclists, but it has some moderately difficult stretches along the way. We will be passing through several of the regions of Spain in order to get a taste of the unique flavors in the different areas.

Spain's roads are usually wide and well surfaced, and Spanish drivers are generally courteous. The drawback to many of Spain's roads is noise. There are only a few quiet roads on the Spanish coast, but where they exist, we will take them. Generally, the farther south you go, the less traveled the roads. If you go inland you will find many more quiet roads, but you will also face cycling the mountains.

Good maps for bicycle touring in Spain are those published by the Instituto Geografico Nacional. Several other European map companies, such as Michelin and Hallweg, also publish usable maps, though none are as detailed as the Michelin maps available for France. Your best buy will be the Ravenstein (RV) series of regional maps at 1:300,000—you'll only need sheets 3/4, 6, and 7/8. If you choose the less detailed Michelin regional maps at 1:400,000, you'll need sheets 443, 445, and 446.

Accommodations

Spain has a tremendous number of camping sites, especially along the eastern coast. It is not uncommon to find a dozen campgrounds within a 3 km stretch of road. Most of the major cities have at least one hostel and a range of hotels. Even in the popular areas, the hostels and hotels fill up only during August.

One of the delights of traveling by bike is visiting and staying in monasteries or convents. Monasteries played an important role in Spain's history, and the country has a large number of them which, permitting vacancies, welcome travelers. Most are in the north of the country. They either charge a modest set fee, or people make donations. The Montserrat monastery near Barcelona, for example, is beautiful, as is Santo Domingo de Silos in Burgos, which first recorded the now-popular Gregorian chants.

Monastery accommodation is usually simple but orderly. The Spanish tourist office has a list of these open monasteries for men and women. Reservations during Lent, Advent, and August are usually necessary. The two monasteries mentioned above need reservations year around. Ask information from your Spanish tourist office.

In the Andalucia province of southern Spain is a system of what are called rural hotels. Located in elaborate settings, these cost as little as pts. 4000 a night and offer a family-run alternative to regular hotels. For more information ask at a Spanish information office or write Asociacion de Hoteles Rurales de Andalucia, Sagunto, 8-atico-3, 04004 Almeria, tel. (they speak English) 34-50-271678.

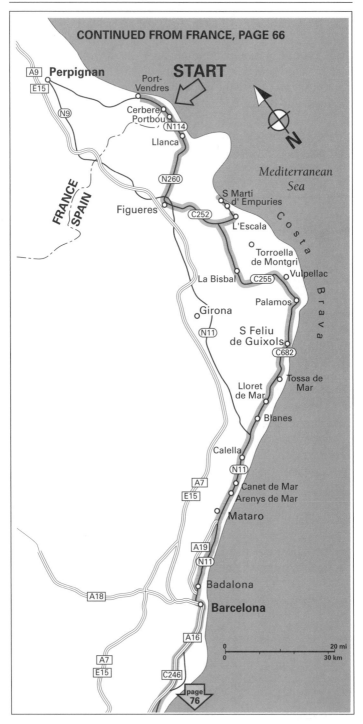

Getting There and Around

Especially during the summer months, there are international flights, including inexpensive charters, from all major European cities to Spain's major airports. You can take several overland routes from France: the flat ride on the Atlantic coast into San Sebastian, the hilly ride that our tour takes on the Costa Brava, or the gorgeous mountainous ride through the Pyrenees. Apart from ferries to the Baleares, Canarias, and Ceuta (a Spanish city on the tip of Morocco), Spain has not been a big sea-faring country since its conquest of the New World. There is a weekly ferry from Barcelona to Marseilles and Livorno, but you're better off with a train if you're not planning to bike.

Spain also does not have a good inter-city bus system in most of the part of the country we are going, so if you want to skip part of the tour, find the train station. The extra charge for taking your bike is much smaller than in other countries and is often free.

Section 1. From Portbou to Barcelona

Distance:	175 km (109 miles)
Terrain:	coastal mix of flat and hills
Duration:	1–3 days
Rating:	difficult

Accommodations

There are hostels, campgrounds and hotels of all categories abound. Good places to stop are Portbou, Figueres, and any of the Costa Brava cities.

1.1 Portbou to La Bisbal

Distance: 77 km (48 miles)

1. Starting on the French frontier station on the eastern coastal road, drop down the N260 for about 3 km into Portbou. It's a much narrower and steeper road than you have been used to on the French side, so ride slowly.

2. Look down to see the rail yard of the city below and the vast expanse of blue sea around you. Welcome to the Costa Brava. If you're used to Latin-American Spanish, the Catalan dialect spoken in the region will sound strange to your ears.

3. Portbou is a pleasant beach town that caters to French tourists. The steep and winding road is a bit intimidating, but with caution you can make the 6 km climb to where you can take a well-deserved rest and admire the view.

4. Descend to the next town, Colera, at the 11 km mark.

5. South of Colera is another steep climb that finishes with a drop into picturesque Llanca.

6. After Llanca, make the comparatively easy climb through the barren mountains. The first peak is at the 19 km mark and the second at the 23 km mark, at which point you descend into a flat farm area.

7. Ride to Figueres through fields of sunflowers and citrus trees on a nice wide road. Figueres is Salvador Dali's home town. Visit the extraordinary Dali museum and relax in the pleasant town. Figueres has camping, a youth hostel, and several inexpensive hotels.

9. From here we want to go southeast, so leave Figueres by way of the national road south.

10. In about 3 km, you see the C252 turnoff to the left for La Bisbal. Continue until you reach La Bisbal (36 km).

1.2 La Bisbal to Barcelona

Distance: 98 km (61 miles)

1. Continue on the same road, which stays flat as you pass farmland, old houses, and campgrounds through the small villages of Vilamacolum, Torroella, and Viladamat. The road is not particularly wide, so keep listening for traffic.

2. About 12 km from La Bisbal, you reach the town of Verges, and shortly thereafter the quaint village of Ultramort.

3. Go through Ultramort, the capital of El Bajo Ampurdán. There's a grand Romanesque palace and a large ceramics factory for you to tour. Ceramics are an important aspect of the economy along the coast.

4. From here, continue straight over the Daro River bridge through Vulpellac on the C255 to Palamos (20 km). The road to Palamos is nicely rolling as you pass the small farming village of Llofriu and nearby Mount Ras, 7 km from Palamos.

5. There's camping 4 km from Palamos, if you don't want to camp on the coast. Go into the center of Palamos. This area is considered the heart of the Costa Brava. Palamos is a good size city with a museum and the 500-year-old Santa Maria church.

6. Head for Sant Feliu de Guixols, about 10 km to the south, by going through the seaside resort of Platja D'Aro.

7. Take the road one block from the beach and continue south. You see the sea again when you come to the bay at Agaro.

8. Go up a hill and then descend to the center of Sant Feliu de Guixols. You will see its castle from the road.

9. The next part of the road is difficult, with many hills on the seaside cliffs, but it is one of the nicest rides in all of Spain.

10. Making sure you have plenty of water, take the narrow and winding road out of Sant Feliu on the C682, climbing to the 43 km marker. It's lovely here.

11. The narrow road continues cutting its way through the mountain as you get alternating glimpses of the green interior and the surrounding blue sea.

12. Pass Canet de Mar and Salions, modern complexes that seem to clash with the rugged natural beauty of the hills.

13. There is a campground near the 28 km marker, but I've seen several people camp by themselves near the road.

14. Tossa is on the 24 km marker. Fom here, follow the signs for Barcelona and Lloret de Mar. The road becomes a bit wider, but it is still hilly.

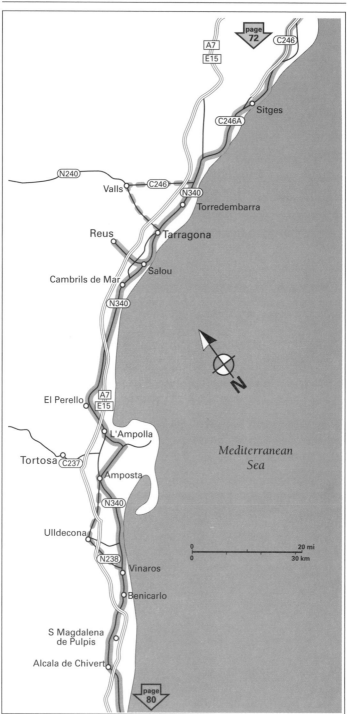

15. Lloret de Mar has a 800-year-old medieval castle on the cliffs above the sea. Here the road becomes more difficult as you pass along hills between the many beach areas.

16. The road smoothes out near Blanes, a good place to break and visit the ruins of a Roman castle. Blanes marks the end of the Costa Brava and the beginning of the Costa El Maresme.

17. Just after Blanes, merge into the N11 and follow it for 59 km into Barcelona. It's a rolling road, easy and wide, but it does have traffic.

18. The towns of Calella and Arenys de Mar along the way are quite nice. You can see Barcelona as you enter its suburbs at Mataro. Signs will direct you around the one-way streets to the city center.

Barcelona and Surroundings

Barcelona is a large and exciting city with an excellent university, famous cathedral, and Antonio Gaudi's fabulous architechure. From here you can visit Montserrat, about 55 km away. You can hear Gregorian chants sung in the Montserrat monastery every Sunday (tel. 93-835-8251 or 835-0251).

Section 2. From Barcelona to Valencia

Distance: 360 km (225 miles)
Terrain: well-paved roads; some small hills
Duration: 3–5 days
Rating: moderate

Accommodations

There are many campgrounds and a variety of hotels in all towns, especially the popular resorts. Good places to stop include Sitges, Tarragona, Miemi, Vinaros, the Castellon area, Sagunto, and Valencia.

2.1 Barcelona to Vinaros

Distance: 215 km (134 miles)

This second part of our tour takes us along the Costa Dorada, the Golden Coast, to Valencia. The ride is moderately easy, with only a few hills as the road goes inland. Most of our trip will be on the main road, which is wide and well paved.

1. To leave Barcelona, simply head south on any one of the main roads toward the airport.

2. Follow the signs for the Viladecansa road, which goes slightly inland and is calmer than the main highway.

3. After the airport, take the C246, a very busy road.

4. Following the signs for Sitges, go inland on the C246 and start going up the mountain, where you'll get an excellent view of the sea.

5. Descend into Sitges, a quaint tourist area with a palm-lined promenade, at approximately the 34 km mark.

6. Take the C246A from Sitges in the direction of Tarragona (55 km from Sitges).

7. About 35 km from Tarragona, the road merges into the C246 and becomes busier.

8. Passing the towns of Cunit and Bellve on your journey, visit the town of Valls, then turn on the N340 and head south.

9. Back on the coastal road, you pass another castle at Criexell, several small towns, and many camping areas. The hilly road follows the sea and is wide with a comfortable shoulder.

10. As you continue south, you will notice the area around you becoming more arid.

11. When you get close to Tarragona, continue to the port and follow the signs for Salou (9 km) on the AP1. This is a fairly quiet road, and Salou is a pleasant and well-known beach town.

12. You can either continue on the same road slightly inland to Reus (9 km) or go down the quiet TV3141 to Cambrils de Mar (10 km), which the locals say is famous for its cuisine.

13. About 3 km from Cambrils de Mar, return to the N340 and ride past the attractive Casa di San José on your right. The road, surrounded by olive and citrus groves, is nice to ride. Spain, not Italy, is the world's largest producer of olive oil and one of the largest producers of citrus. Cars make up most of the traffic on this predominately flat road parallel to the railroad.

14. The next town, Miami Platja, caters to foreign tourists and is a good place to exchange money.

15. Take the hill toward El Perello, where you will see a small, unmarked side road on your right just after the 1108 km marker leads through an olive grove for about 2 km into El Perello. The northern section of the town is old and interesting. You probably will be hot and tired, and this is a good place to relax, refill your supplies, and then get back on the N340.

16. The next town is L'Ampolla, 7 km downhill from El Perelló.

17. At the overpass to the expressway, take the local road to Amposta (174 km from Valencia). Cross a beautiful bridge over the Ebro river and enter the lovely old town. You have a choice of returning to the N340 on a relatively flat but busy road, or taking the smaller but hilly road to Ulldecona (18 km) and Vinaros (16 km).

18. The N340 between Amposta and Vinaros is wide, well-surfaced, and less trafficked than other parts of the road. If the wind is with you, you can fly. South of St. Charles you take a hill, and the road remains mildly rolling for a few km. Take the local road into Vinaros.

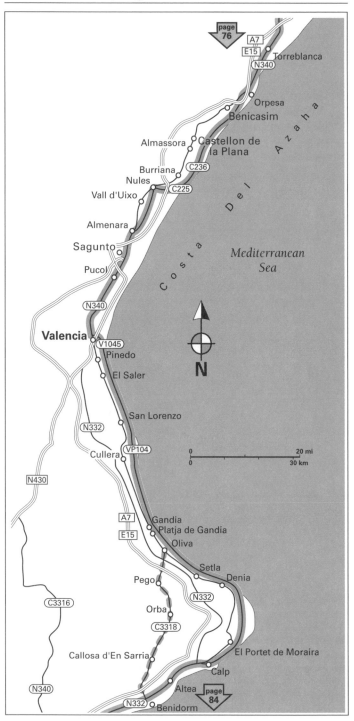

2.2 Vinaros to Valencia

Distance: 145 km (91 miles)

1. From Vinaros, it's another 7 km to Benicarlo, a lively though not particularly pretty tourist area. When you go inland you climb, then when you return to the sea you descend.

2. Santa Magdalena de Pulpis is a quaint small town and a good place to tour the narrow streets and rest beneath the trees. There's also a public swimming pool.

3. Alcala de Chivert is another graceful town along the way.

4. Continue south, passing olive and fruit trees, and in 13 km you reach Torreblanca.

5. The road comes to an end for us at Orpesa (15 km), a town built upon a rock. Go under the expressway and, at the top of the hill, turn left onto the smaller coastal road. It rises just enough to give you a view of the mountains before descending to a pleasant resort area. We're back to a scenic area where Spaniards come for holiday. It's a good time to go for a swim after a long ride.

6. Follow the white signs for Castellon de la Plana, rather than the ones leading back to the N340. Our route takes us along the coast.

7. In Castellon de la Plana, go around El Grao (shore), and ask people for the road to Almassora since it's hard to find.

8. In the central residential part of Almassora you come to a roundabout with a sign for the C236 to Burriana (6 km). Pass over the Rio Mijares through farm land. An old church and castle dominate Burriana.

9. Now follow the signs for Nules (6 km) on the C225 from the center of Burriana.

10. Cross over the Autopista to arrive at Nules, a wonderful city with several refreshing water fountains.

11. From here, continue on the C225 to Vall d'Uixó and then drop down to the N340 at Almenara, or stay on the

N340. On the rocky hills inland you see the remains of two towers.

12. Cross over the usually dry Rio Palancia to arrive in Sagunto. The town has a Roman theater, a good museum, and some worthwhile historic sights like the old Jewish Quarter.

13. From Sagunto, follow a local road on the east side of the train track back to Pucol (5 km).

14. Go through the center of Pucol. Now the ride is straight and smooth through the villages all the way to Valencia.

Valencia

Spain's third-largest city, Valencia was one of the most important centers during Spain's conquest of the New World. The city is loaded with history and religious art and is a lively place with fashionable stores and gathering places for young people. The coast around Valencia, with its long sandy beaches, is one of the nicest we will encounter during our tour.

Section 3. From Valencia to Alicante

Distance: 185 km (115 miles)
Terrain: scenic route
Duration: 2–3 days
Rating: moderate with one hilly section

Accommodations

There are many places to stay, especially between Valencia and Cullera as well as close to Alicante.

3.1 Valencia to Gandia

Distance: 63 km (39 miles)

The next phase of our trip, from Valencia to Alicante on the Costa del Azaha, to the Orange Blossom Coast, and finally to the Costa Blanca, is wonderfully scenic with comparatively little traffic. Only the central section of our trip is difficult. Don't depend on the signs when you are ready to leave Valenica; ask for directions because the area is so large and confusing for the newcomer (part of the bicycle touring experience).

1. Leaving Valencia, follow the river road—not the one in the center of town that has been converted into a park—down to the beach of Nazaret, then turn right on the coastal road. Don't aim for the national roads near Valencia because they are all highways.

2. Take the V1045 coastal road to Pinedo. Soon the road becomes the VP104 to El Saler (10 km).

3. Ask for the road to the popular discoteca called Canal. It's a flat suburban road with houses, gardens, farmland, sandy beaches, and camping.

4. The road continues along the flat coast all the way to San Lorenzo, about 33 km from the Valencia port. There are beaches all along the way that are frequented mainly by the locals.

5. After San Lorenzo, there is a medium-grade climb to Cullera. Descend to the Júcar River and stay along the coast.

6. Continue along the coast to the Gandia area. Gandia, the main city, sits on a river that nourishes the plain and the orange trees which grow in the area.

3.2 Gandia to Alicante

Distance: 122 km (76 miles)

In Gandia, ask someone how to locate the local road to Oliva. This part of the road is flat and offers good riding.

From Oliva, you have two options, staying along the coast or going inland through Pego (which has a fun zoo) and Callosa d'En Sarria. The coastal road is rough, but the inland route on the C3318, which reaches almost 1000 m, is even more challenging. Both are scenic, but if you're in good shape you may want to try the inland route.

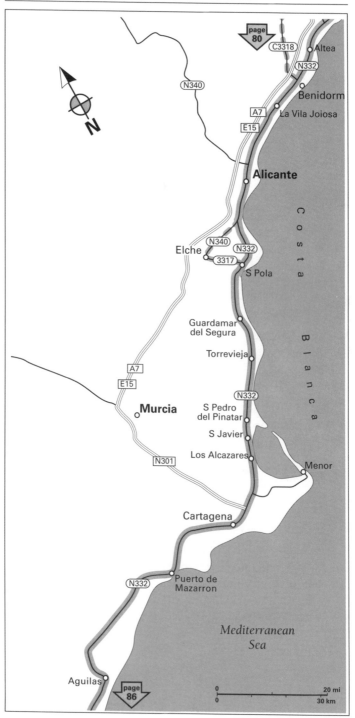

A. Inland Route from Oliva to Benidorm

1. The inland road begins to climb as soon as you leave Oliva, but the grade is light until you reach Pego.

2. After Pego, the climb is hard, with only a few downhill grades on a narrow winding road until you get to Sagra.

3. It's mildly hilly to Orba, then you go down to a bridge and climb again to Coll de Rates.

4. The road is difficult all the way to Callosa d'En Sarria, which you reach after a 10 km descent.

5. Just off the road near Callosa d'En Sarria are the impressive Algar waterfalls.

6. You climb again, descend again, then hit La Nucia. The rest of the road to the coast at Benidorm is easy.

B. Coastal Route from Oliva to Benidorm

1. From Oliva, take the road just to the east of the national road that leads to Setla and then to Denia (33 from Gandia). Denia has a castle on a cliff overlooking both sea and town and some nice secluded beaches.

2. Continue south on the winding uphill coastal road to the San Antonio highland, and descend into Xabea.

3. From Xabea, a sprawling, not very pretty town, begin a 7 km scenic climb to Benitachell, then a 6 km descent to El Portet de Moraira, a fishing town.

4. From here, it's a pleasant and easy 11 km beach ride to Calp.

5. To get back to the N332, 4 km away, you face a 1 km climb that includes a long tunnel followed by a beautiful view, and then you arrive at the main road for Altea.

6. At Altea, proceed on the left of the road down to the sea or go up the hill overlooking the town, and continue into Benidorm, a few km away. This is where we meet up with those who followed the more strenuous inland route.

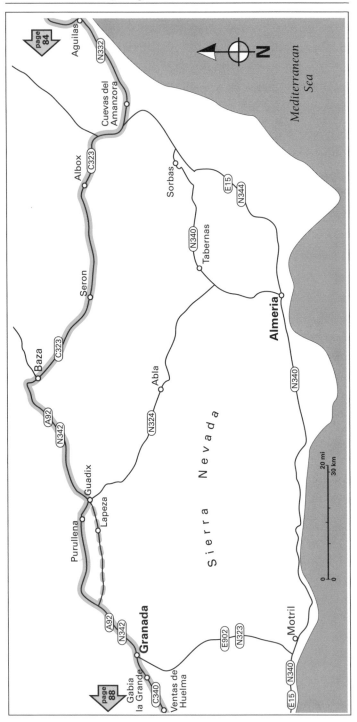

Continuation of Route

1. From Benidorm, follow the coastal road to La Vila Joiosa, a prosperous fishing town.

2. After La Vila Joiosa there are rolling hills until you reach the road leading to Busot. At that intersection make a left, following the signs for the *playa*.

3. The beach road passes Albufereta, and soon you are in Alicante.

Alicante

This is one of the nicest cities that we will be visiting. Founded over 2000 years ago, Alicante has several historic sites, but it is also a fashionable and attractive modern city with a renowned promenade.

Section 4. From Alicante to Tarifa

Distance: 704 km (440 miles)
Terrain: rugged dry mountains inland, then
               rolling coast
Duration: 6–10 days
Rating: Some sections are very difficult

Accommodations

Inland between Cartagena and Granada you can find hotels only in the larger towns, but the coastal area is flooded with accommodations. Places to stop include Aguilas, Cuevas del Amanzora, Baza, Guadix, Granada, and in the many communities of the Costa del Sol.

4.1 Alicante to Granada

Distance: 370 km (231 miles)

1. When you're ready to leave Alicante, take the main road marked to the airport. This is not a good cycling road, but after only a few km you reach the N340 to Elche and Murcia.

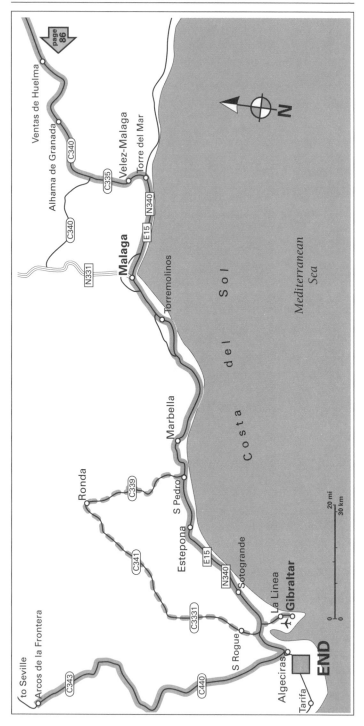

2. Elche, where the famous carving of the Dama de Elche was discovered, has the nicest park in Spain.

3. Continue on the N332 past El Alfet on a mostly flat road to Santa Pola, 18 km from Alicante. This is a fishing village, and you can go down to the cape and see the harbor and the beach. Off in the distance is the small island of Tabarca.

4. The road continues flat but pretty for the next 15 km to Guardamar del Segura and Torrevieja, another 15 km.

5. Get off the N332 on the first exit signed for the "playa," and continue along the smaller coastal road since it is the more scenic.

6. Exit at Torrevieja and continue on N332 past La Zenia and Dehesa to the popular beach area of San Pedro del Pinatar. In summer this area is quite hot and traffic increases significantly. But off-season, the road is calm, hilly, and relatively easy. There are more traces of Arab influence in this part of Spain, not only in the monuments but also in the social customs.

7. Go another 38 km to Cartagena, passing Los Alcazares and a few more resort areas on the Mar Menor.

8. Cartagena, probably named because it was founded by Carthage, is now a naval base. The old cathedral, before it was destroyed in Spain's Civil War, was the oldest church in the country.

9. Right after you cross the Rio Almanzora, climb up slightly to a turnoff for Cuevas del Amanzora and take the road marked for Zurgena and Canteras for about 5 km.

10. Follow the small road for 11 km until you reach the end. The first part of the road is easy, but at the end there is a hill.

11. Turn right in the direction of Zurgena. From here you have a hilly road for 8 km. Descend into Zurgena, then go uphill for another km to the end of the road.

12. Turn right, and you'll be on the C323 heading to Baza. This road is easy until after Seron, 50 km away, at which point it becomes quite hilly for another 30 km to Baza.

13. The next part of the road to Guadix, 915 m high, is also hilly, but you face no serious grades. About 20 km out of Baza is the worst hill, and about 3 km from Guadix there is another good climb. The road is moderately busy but wide.

14. Continue on the N342 for Granada, where the main road has three major passes to ascend. There's an alternative if you want to take a slightly easier road: 5 km outside Guadix, take the left turnoff for Lugros and Purullena. Follow the local road to Lapeza, 12 km away.

15. The next 25 km stretch between Lapeza and the main road at Pinos Genil is lonely and hilly, but it is a wonderful ride.

16. When you reach the end of the road, turn right toward Cenes, and in a few easy km you're in Granada.

Granada

This may be Spain's most interesting city, with the Alhambra in all its splendor, and the shops, churches and lovely gardens. Stay in a hotel downtown to tour the city, and when you are ready to leave, continue south on the Camino de Ronda toward the airport.

4.2 Granada to Malaga

Distance: 180 km (112 miles)

1. Leaving Granada toward the airport, take the quiet C340 for over 70 km.

2. The first 16 km to Mala passes the grey village of Gabia la Grande and is the most physically taxing.

3. Descend into Mala, then take the road to Ventas de Huelma, 10 km away.

4. From there, continue following the C340 to Agron and the Pantano de Bermejales.

5. After this point, the road climbs quite a bit to the large city of Alhama de Granada.

6. You must climb again to the 920 m pass at Pto. de Zafarraya. It's 16 km up and down to Ventas de Zafarraya.

7. The rest of the road down to the coast, 30 km away, is easy and fun.

8. Eleven km south of Ventas de Zafarraya, change over to the C335 for Velez-Malaga and Torre del Mar.

9. Reaching a coastal road, the N340, stay on it until you reach Malaga, which has a large British community, as does the entire area around the city.

4.3 Malaga to Tarifa

Distance: 154 km (96 miles)

1. From Malaga, take the N340 east, and go 60 km to Marbella, a newly developed area, passing Torremolinos and Fuengirola along a scenic stretch overlooking the sea.

2. Continue on the main road via San Pedro, Estepona, and Sotogrande toward San Rogue and Algeciras.

3. The main road wraps around the bay with some great views of Gibraltar, to Algeciras on the western side of the bay.

4. Our tour continues along the N340, 23 km down to Tarifa along a winding, hilly road with several long tunnels and great views. Tarifa is considered the wind surfing capital of Europe because of the constant wind that rips through the Strait of Gibraltar.

Sidetrips

It is a good idea to combine this section of the tour with one or more of the following four sidetrips. It's like four mini-vacations to different worlds, though all within cycling distance from each other.

Sidetrip to Ronda

From San Pedro, there's a hard mountainous road, the C339, from here to Ronda, further inland. Going over three major passes for 50 km, it is a great ride through the mountains. You can get back to the coast between San Rogue and Algeciras along the equally spectacular but much longer C 41—about 100 km.

Sidetrip to Gibraltar

To visit Gibraltar, turn left toward La Linea and Gibraltar after Sotogrande, shortly before you reach San Roque. Gibraltar is a wonderful city with mock British shops and policemen and a huge steep rock that you can bike up for a great view. Much of the historic interest here is war related.

Sidetrip to North Africa

From Algeciras, you can take a ferry to North Africa. There are services to Tangier, Ceuta, and Melilla. Many people take the ferry to Ceuta, which is under Spanish control, and then ride to the border into Morocco.

Sidetrip to Seville

If you would like to go on to Seville, continue another 40 km going northwest on the N340, and then take the hilly local road through Arcos de la Frontera or continue another 40 km and take the national road next to the Autopista at Cadiz. This road is easier but more crowded, and the climate along both routes is hot and dry. Either way takes you a distance of some 240 km before you reach Seville.

Chapter 6
Greece

Greece, with its history, beauty, seaside resorts, traditional mountain villages, and wonderful people, is a favorite place for cyclists to ride. Near the coast, the roads are moderately hilly but wide and smooth. The inland route is very mountainous and quite strenuous. Greece has three national highways: one that runs from Athens to Thessaloniki and to the northern border, another that traverses the country from Patras to Athens, and a third which goes from Corinth down the Peloponnese to Tripoli. These roads are busy in summer, but they are often in better condition than the secondary inland roads.

The most intense traffic is around the greater Athens area since that is where a third of the population lives. Roads are well marked, and the major routes have signs written in both Greek and English. If you need information on road conditions, try the Automobile and Touring Club (ELPA), phone: 779-1615.

Greece is a nation of hundreds of islands, most of which are small and only have a principal town with little room for biking. In addition to this tour of the mainland, I have chosen four of the larger islands away from the mainland

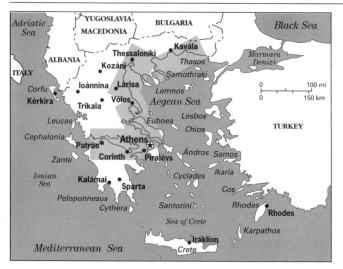

for riding, covered in separate chapters: Crete (Chapter 13), Rhodes, Karpathos, and Samos (Chapter 14), which can be used as a jumping off point to or from Turkey.

Often when you hear someone talking about Greece, the word "ancient" is attached to it. Certainly our civilization owes a tremendous debt to these ancients, in the arts as well as in our government. People travel to Greece for its history, its beaches, and its cuisine. Greeks are a traditional people in general and, quite understandably, appreciate it when you respect their religion and act with dignity. It is wise not to get drunk, use drugs, or dress differently than the natives.

Many people either fly into Athens or take a ferry to a principal port or one of the islands. Bargain flights in and out of Greece are widely available. Our tour originates from Brindisi, Italy, by way of the ferry, but ferries from Bari, Ancona, Cyprus, Istanbul, and Alexandria also exist. The main Greek port is Pireas, a short ride from Athens.

Greece has become much more expensive in recent years but remains one of the cheapest EEC countries in which to travel. With many campgrounds, about two dozen youth hostels, and simple hotels as cheap as $10 a night, Greece has ample accomodations for the budget traveler, but do-it-yourself camping is prohibited. Meals in simple tavernas cost about $5–10, while food stores will keep you well stocked along any ride for less. Ferries to the islands are also inexpensive—for example, $20 deck class and $35 cabin class, to Crete.

Maps are available locally only in the major cities. One suitable series of maps are those published by Freytag & Berndt, which cover the country, including all the islands, in 15 sheets, and are detailed enough for cycling, or the same company's regional series (you'll need sheets 2, 3, 4, and 5). The double-sided Ravenstein (RV) country map at 1:300,000 is the best bargain around, covering the entire country (but not all the islands) on one double-sided sheet.

Be prepared for some confusion in the spelling of placenames. Since the Greek script is not always easy to transcribe into Roman letters, you will often find varying spellings for the same place names. What is written with a *K* may be with a *C* elsewhere, a *Y* may become an *I*, an *E* may turn out te be *AI*, and *H* or *X* may become *CH*.

Overview of the Route Through Greece

Connecting with our tour of southern Italy, the ferry from Brindisi takes you to Patras, a scenic coastal city that will be the starting point for this tour. To avoid the mountains that await inland travelers, we will primarily stay on the coastal roads, with a few optional trips inland for the well-conditioned biker. As always, feel free to adapt this tour to suit your own strengths and interests.

View of typical Greek island port city.

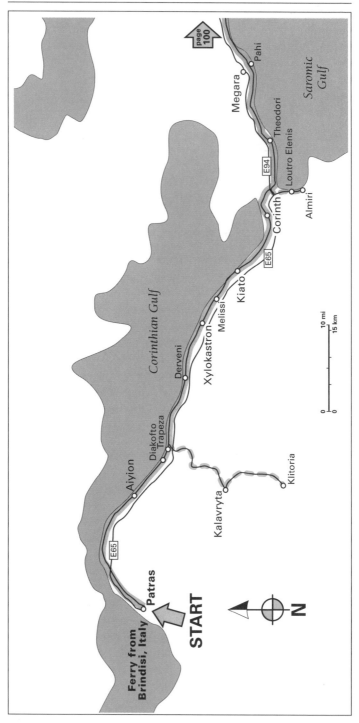

If, instead of landing at Patras by ferry, you fly into Athens, skip the first section and start your tour with Section 2. Even so, it will be worthwile to backtrack and at least use the second part of this tour in reverse order to visit Corinth from Athens, since it is one of the truly great attractions.

Section 1. From Patras to Athens

Distance: 215 km (134 miles)
Terrain: mostly seaside
Duration: 2–3 days
Rating: easy

Accommodations

Along this route, you are never more than a few km away from a hotel or a campground. Get a list of hotels and campgrounds at any Greek tourist office.

Patras

Patras is the largest city of the Peloponnese and offers ferry service to the Ionian islands of Kefallinia, Paxi, and Corfu. Perched on a hill, the old part of the city is full of quaint houses and shops. The archaeological museum on Mesonos Street is worth visiting as is the church of Ayios Andreas. Today Patras is important as a center for shipping and business. There are some campgrounds nearby; if your ferry lands in the afternoon, you may want to stop at Ayia Patron (6 km from the port) for the night, or rest in the city's hostel.

1.1 From Patras to Corinth

Distance: 135 km (84 miles)

1. When you leave the port, turn left and follow the signs for Athens.

2. Take a small hill on a busy road next to a service road. Don't be alarmed about the rugged climb; this hill is the last until we near Athens.

3. Do not take the National Highway; instead find the local road close to the sea.

4. Beginning at Agia, follow the sign left for Rio (8 km) at the 209 km mark, where you will see a ruined castle. The ride ahead is incredibly attractive as you pedal between the calm blue water and the green pine-covered mountains.

5. Along our coastal road to Corinth, you will find at least four well-marked campgrounds. The train tracks are always near. You will find several lovely beaches and resorts to greet you along the way to Rio.

6. The next large town is Egion (also written Aiyion, 43 km. from Patras). It is a pretty tourist region with camping near the sea. If you're interested in shrines, ask directions to the chapel of the Virgin Trypiti, carved into the side of a nearby mountain.

7. After Egion, continue on the slightly hilly road toward the villages of Trapeza and Platanos (note sidetrip to Kalavryta).

8. Back on the coastal road, pass Derveni, Kamari, and the popular resort of Xylokastron, which has camping near the beach.

9. Proceed to Sikia, Melissi, Diminio, and Kiato, a large modern town where you can buy supplies.

10. Heading further on the coastal road, pass Velo, Kokoni, Vrahati, Assos, and Perigiali before reaching Corinth.

Corinth

The ancient city of Corinth is a must for travelers. Plan to spend at least a couple of hours visiting the ruins, which include a temple of Apollo, a theater, an agora, and a museum. You can walk around the ruins before climbing to the top of the Acrocorinth rock (550 m altitude) for a panoramic view.

Sidetrip to Kalavryta

Just before Trapeza is a side trip for the hearty cyclist. Simply go past the town of Diakofto and take the road on the right leading to Kalavryta. This is a mountainous area, full of natural beauty and fascinating villages, but it's a tough climb. Those interested in caves should go to Kastria and see the 2 km long cave of the lakes. A short distance past the caves are the the beautiful villages of Klitoria and Aroania, high above the sea. This lush area is in contrast to the dry mountains we generally associate with Greece.

1.2 Corinth to Athens

Distance 88 km (55 miles)

1. Go through the uninspiring city of modern Corinth to reach the National Highway, a wide and safe road.

2. For an optional side trip, you can make a right turn at the sign for Kiravrsi, which has the ruins of a sanctuary of Poseidon, and head further south along the Saronic Gulf to Loutro Elenis, which has hot springs.

3. Otherwise, continue straight until you come to a strip of tourist shops followed by the Corinthian Canal, a century-old excavation that separates the Peloponnese from the rest of Greece.

4. Crossing the bridge is definitely a thrill as you look down through the cut rock into the deep blue chasm of the sea below.

5. Right after the canal, take the right-hand exit leading back to the small coastal road.

6. The coast as you head south is quite different from the parts of Greece you have ridden through previously. In this section of the tour, the towns are more industrial and not as well inhabited, and the coastal road becomes hillier as you approach Athens.

7. Eleusis, a large industrial city 70 km from Corinth, is the home of the ancient temple to Demeter and has other interesting ruins.

8. Just east of Eleusis, the local road ends, and you must rejoin the National Highway, which is hilly and dense with traffic.

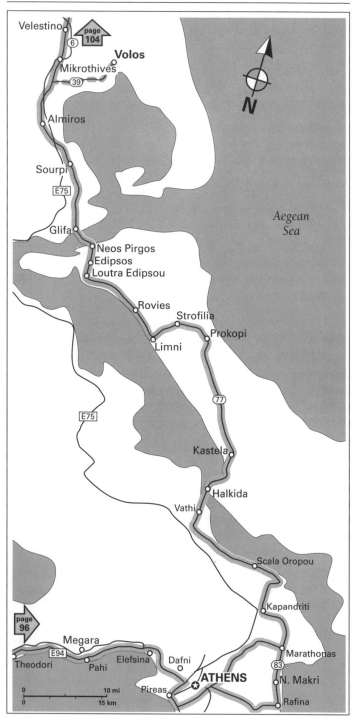

9. Continue uphill and around the bay to Dafni and visit its splendid monastery—probably the most important Byzantine church in the world. Camping is nearby.

10. From here, Athens is only 20 km away; you will start seeing the legendary orange smog hovering over the valley before the city itself comes into view.

11. Keep going straight along the busy road, called both Leoforos Athinon and Leoforos Kavalas, and head for the center of the city.

Athens

As well as having a tremendous number of ruins and museums to see, Athens is a lively modern city with diverse neighborhoods. Have your guidebook of the city handy so you can visit the spots that interest you the most. The Plaka and Monastiraki districts have hostels and inexpensive hotels. Cycling in the center of town is no different from cycling in any other bustling city, so be on your guard for fast turning cars.

After spending a comfortable few days in Athens, seeing the sights, eating at tavernas, and mixing with the hustle of the city, prepare to move on to the next part of our tour.

Head north toward Thessaloniki by way of the eastern coastal road, as opposed to taking the rather taxing route inland through Thebes and Delphi. There are two ways to leave Athens, both of which end at Marathonas. I'll describe them both and let you choose. Unfortunately, all roads out of Athens are absolutely no fun, and you won't miss much if you put your bike on a bus for the first 20 km out of the city.

Section 2. From Athens to Halkida

Distance: 90–110 km (56–68 miles)
Terrain: dry mountains
Duration: 1–2 days
Rating: slightly difficult

Accommodations

Every town has at least one hotel.

2.1 Athens to Marathonas

Distance : 42–50 km (26–31 miles)

You get to choose between two routes out of Athens. Route A is longer but may be marginally easier.

Route A. Going North Through Kifissia

1. Ride from the centrally located Sindagma Square, and go east up the hill to Vassilissis Sofias Street.

2. Follow this busy street straight to Kifissia, about 15 km from Sindagma, and the traffic begins to thin out. You pass a stadium, the Athens Hilton, and the American Embassy on this road, and you see signs for Lamia, Thessaloniki, and the Olympic Stadium as well.

3. Just ask for directions to Kifissia along the way if you become confused. There's camping at Kifissia on the other side of the National Highway.

4. It's uphill all the way until past Kiffissia.

5. The road is unmarked until you come to Ekali, 18 km from Athens and about 250 m high.

6. The road becomes smaller and quieter as you begin to descend. Shortly after, there's an intersection to Dionissos (4 km) and Makri (15 km on a hilly road).

7. At Anixi, the next town, ask for directions to Agios Stefanos and from there follow the signs for Marathonas Lake. The beauty of this area is reason for taking this route, which has a terrific overlook for viewing the breaktaking pine moutains and lake below.

8. Go over a narrow old bridge/dam, 8 km from Marathonas, then wind around and climb 3 km before descending toward the sleepy village of Marathonas.

Route B. Going East to Marathonas

This route for leaving Athens is less difficult than the first, but equally busy.

1. Beginning at the same road, Vasilissis Sofias, turn right about 3 blocks after the American Embassy to Fidipidou

Street, which later becomes Mesogeion Street, and follow the signs for Marathonas.

2. The road at this point is a divided highway and takes you through the urban area to less than 200 m above sea level at about the 14 km mark.

3. Right after, there's a roundabout at Stavros. From here, continue straight to Rafina.

4. The road descends through the Palini/Gerakas area.

5. Rafina, at the 25 km mark, is 3 km from the beach where there's camping, a hostel, and boats to nearby islands.

6. At the 34 km mark, you encounter the turnoff for Dionissos, 10 km, and Ekali, 15 km.

7. Along this route, you reach Marathonas, appropriately enough, after having cycled approximately a marathon—42 km. The distance of the first option, Route A, is closer to 50 km.

2.2 Marathonas to Halkida

Distance: 47 km (29 miles)

1. From the center of Marathonas, follow the signs to Kapandriti, 20 km away.

2. The 7 km to Gramatiko and another 7 km to Varnavas are both fairly strenuous climbs on a nice road.

3. Continue to Kapandriti, 7 km, and 10 km to the north, Kalamos.

4. From Kalamos, take the pleasant road to Amphiareion en route to Oropos. About 4 km from Kalamos, after a right curve, you come to a road which leads downhill to the entrance to the Amphiareion ruins. None of the uphill grades past Marathonas are too difficult. Enjoy the pleasant ride through the quiet towns.

5. Head back to Scala Oropou on the north coast, and follow the flat coastal road to Halkoutsi, Dilessi, and Paralia Avlidas, about 30 km from Kalamos. The road is open, smooth, and quiet, and these towns are relaxed and pleasant.

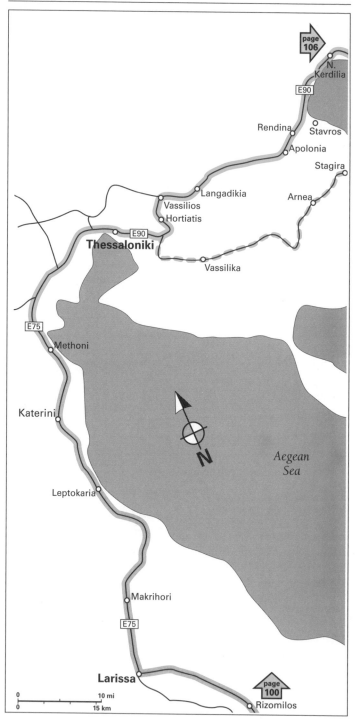

6. Go past Vathi and turn right when the road ends.

7. Follow the sign to Halkida (Chalkis), and bear left as you continue north on Route 77.

Section 3. From Halkida to Thessaloniki

Distance: 418 km (261 miles)
Terrain: mixed hills and flats
Duration: 3–6 days
Rating: moderate, with a few difficult sections

Accommodations

All main cities have a range of hotels, and there are campgrounds near our route.

3.1 Halkida to Larissa

Distance: 265 km (165 miles)

1. Leave Halkida on Route 77 going north.

2. After 6 km you reach the town of Kastela, where the road becomes slightly hilly.

3. Go a short distance to Prokopi, and from there on to the quiet village of Strofilia.

4. Take the left fork in the road to the fishing village of Limni.

5. There is a campground at Rovies, 8 km north along an attractive pebble beach.

6. Continue on a nice road to Edipsos, a pleasant resort city with thermal baths and some ancient ruins.

7. Ride another few km to Neos Pirgos, where you can take the half-hour ferry ride to Glifa.

8. Back on the mainland, begin going north on the local road that parallels the National Highway.

9. Pass Sourpi, cross the highway, and come to the town of Almiros, 40 km from Glifa. The first part of the trip is hilly, but the majority of the ride is flat.

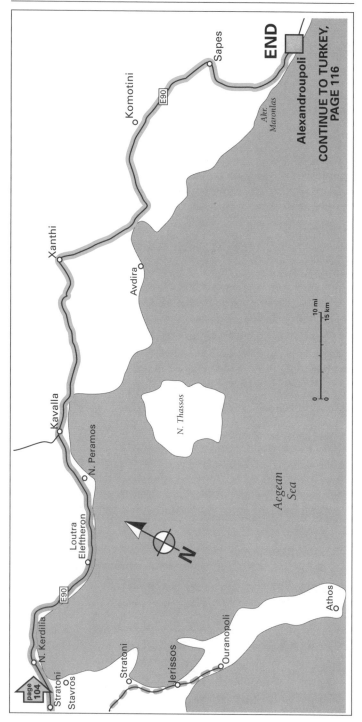

CONTINUE TO TURKEY, PAGE 116

END

Alexandroupoli

Akr. Maronias

Sapes

Komotini

E90

Xanthi

Avdira

N. Thassos

Aegean Sea

Kavalla

N. Peramos

Loutra Eleftheron

N. Kerdilia

E90

N

Stratoni
Stavros

Stratoni

Jerissos

Ouranopoli

Athos

page 104

10 mi
15 km

10. The road continues north past Krokio and underneath the National Highway to Mikrothives. From here you may go to Volos and take a ferry to the Sporades Islands, or you may cycle along the coast to the beaches.

11. Our route continues north by following the signs for Larissa. Merge into the road to Larissa.

12. Exit at Kokaleika, and then continue north another 6 km to Velestino.

13. Cycle the 40 km to Larissa by staying on the local Route 6 that traverses Rizomilos and Armenion. Larissa is a pleasant place to stop for the night.

3.2 Larissa to Thessaloniki

Distance: 153 km (95 miles)

1. From Larissa, take the National Highway north toward Thessaloniki.

2. The next major city is Katerini, a good place to stop and relax. There are several wooded areas off the coastal road that are ideal for a picnic lunch.

3. At Katerini, take the local road next to the National Highway for about 30 km.

4. Get back on the highway at Methoni (there are a couple of campgrounds nearby) and continue to Thessaloniki,

Thessaloniki

This is Greece's second-largest city, and has been inhabited for more than 2000 years. This sophisticated center of commerce with its renowned university offers visitors a variety of activities: modern shops, ruins such as the Arch of Galerius, churches, and festivities. The Folklore Museum houses traditional costume and crafts, and the church of Panaghia Akheiropoietos is one of the oldest in the world. From the port, you can take ferries to Lemnos, Lesbos, Hios, and other islands.

Sidetrip to Mt. Athos

If you are male and interested in monastic life and religious art from the Byzantine era, Mt. Athos should be on your itinerary. An area of profound natural beauty, Mt. Athos is a separate state, and you need special permission to visit. Your application to enter is processed formally; inquire at your Greek consulate for entry details, and make preparations before leaving home. Take your permission to the Directorate of Civil Affairs in Thessaloniki (tel: 031–270–092). You cannot cycle inside the monastery area.

Sidetrip to Ouranopolis

You don't have to be male for this trip. Part of the area is wooded, and you pass vineyards and rustic villages on this at times extremely hilly road. Ride to the town of Arnea, and from Arnea go south to Megali, Panagia, and Gomati. This is a handsome, verdant area. We begin seeing the mountains of Athos from Lerissos. On the way back, go up the coast to Stratoni, then head inland up to Stagira, Aristotle's home town, before continuing north along the coastal road toward Kavala.

Section 4. From Thessaloniki to the Turkish Border

Distance:	380 km (237 miles)
Terrain:	coast and rolling hills
Duration:	3–5 days
Rating:	moderately easy

This last part of our Greek tour, from Thessaloniki to the Turkish border, is a pleasant and quiet coastal ride.

Accommodations

This area has fewer tourist facilities, so plan your day to end at the larger towns such as Amfipolis, Kavalla, Xanthi, Komotini or Alexandroupoli.

4.1 Thessaloniki to Kavalla

Distance: 163 km (101 miles)

It's possible for many cyclists to do this part of the trip in one day since, except for the beginning, it's an easy road, made even easier by a light breeze coming off the sea.

1. From Thessaloniki, take the main road, E90, go up Mt. Hortiatis to Panorama, and then cycle another 14 km to the main road at Ag. Vassilios. This is about the only hilly area of the trip.

2. On the main road you will pass the villages of Langadikia (11 km), Stivos, Apolonia, and Rendina, before reaching the shore, about 75 km from Thessaloniki.

3. There are camping facilities at the shore.

4. Pass by the scenic Lakes Volvi and Koronia.

5. Wind around the shore to Kavalla, about 160 km from Thessaloniki

Kavala

Kavala is a medium-size port city dominated by a hillside fort. There is camping on both sides of the town and a

Typical Greek Orthodox church.

variety of other accommodations as well. Ferries to other islands, including nearby Thassos, are available.

4.2 Kavalla to the Turkish Border

Distance: 217 km (135 miles)

1. From Kavalla, head inland by staying on the main road west and passing the towns of Xanthi and Komotini.

2. Stay on this road until, 180 km from Kavalla, you drop down to the coast at Alexandroupoli. En route, you will see a few nice churches, large bird nests sitting atop telephone poles, beaches, and many villages.

3. This area was Turkish until 1912, a fact you are reminded of as you also begin seeing the signs of Islamic influence. This is a quiet and relaxing ride, but feel free to leave our route for side trips to the ancient port of Avdira, 26 km south of Xanthi, and Maronia, 32 km south of Komotini.

4. Unlike the other cities that we have passed, Alexandroupoli has an unwelcoming feel and a heavy military presence. However, this unexciting city offers us our final overnight stopping point in Greece, with hotels and camping facilities.

5. There are no towns near the frontier, another 43 km away.

If you are continuing into Turkey, present your passport on the Greek side of the border, cross the bridge, go inside the Turkish customs building and get ready for a different kind of trip than what you have experienced so far. See Chapter 7 for details.

Chapter 7
Turkey

Turkey is a large country with many difficult mountain passes awaiting the intrepid touring cyclist. It's a fascinating, beautiful ride and much less difficult if you follow a coastal route.

Getting There

Turkey is accessible in many respects: it has road, ferry, and air connections to fit into just about any arrangement or budget. You can take the road from Greece described in the previous chapter, or take one of the ferry connections from the Greek mainland to Istanbul. Ferries also run from nearby Greek islands to the Turkish coast: Rhodes to Marmaris, Samos to Kusadasi, Cos to Bodrum, Chios to Cesme, and Lesbos to Ayvalik. Hydrofoils to Turkey from these islands cost about $25 including port taxes, and you often need to leave your passport at a travel agency overnight. There are ferries from the Turkish part of Cyprus as well as road connections from all neighboring countries. Istanbul, Ankara, Antalya, and Konya are served by

international flights. In December, Konya features a special festival of whirling dervishes. Trains to and around Turkey are not good, although the famous Orient Express to Istanbul is back in service.

No prior visas are required for Americans, but British and Irish tourists may be made to pay for a visa on arrival, about $8. The Turkish authorities will stamp your passport on entry, and you can go anywhere in the country. However, the Kurdish area near the eastern border is unstable, and diplomatic advice should be sought before trying to enter. The Turkish army will probably stop you from entering if there is any sign of instability.

If you are feeling adventurous, don't limit your riding to the tour described here. The interior of Turkey includes wonderful places such as Cappadocia that are fascinating, albeit mountainous, areas to ride.

Suitable maps for the coastal regions of Turkey (where our tour concentrates) are readily available in most European countries, while in the United States, you can at least get American Map/Langenscheidt Euro Cart or Ravenstein's Turkey West and Turkey East maps, which show reasonable detail, considering their scale of 1:800,000. Some maps of Greece also show just enough of Turkey to help you on your way.

Turkey is an inexpensive country for foreigners. Although the country's finances seem from our perspective to be in a state of ruin, with an astounding inflation rate and high unemployment due to a rapidly increasing population, Turkey is a model economy for the young Asian states of the former Soviet Union. Although not a rich country, Turkey is industrially developed and has a strong infrastructure, including wide roads and relatively little traffic outside the main cities. As you move east and inland, the population seems poorer and the country less developed. Even the coastal roads our tour takes are not always in good shape, but you get used to being bounced around on occasion.

Our tour concentrates on the most developed parts of the country, so you will pass tourist areas with hotels and campgrounds and cities where you can eat a meal in a modest restaurant for less than $5. Not every hotel or restaurant is as clean as you might wish, particularly in the smaller towns, so be prepared to use your sleeping bag in small towns. Bring a mosquito coil since they are hard to find here. There is also a lack of garbage disposal facilities, and the side of the road often takes the place of a public litter bin. Bottled water is available, and the cuisine is cheap and delicious. The tourist areas have English-speaking tourist offices that will help with lists of accommodations.

Local Customs

Turkey is an Islamic culture, but since WWI has become more secularized than other Muslim countries. The written language was changed from Arabic script to Latin script by Ataturk, the father of the Turkish state, who also modernized other aspects of the Ottoman Empire and is now revered by the Turks.

However, as a westerner you will find the country's moral values very traditional, even archiac, especially in light of the comparatively limited role women still play in their society. Fortunately foreign women are not expected to follow the same code. In general, restrain your behavior somewhat and you will not offend; the local people are hospitable and will treat both men and women travelers well.

In the tourist areas, which our tour passes through in parts, be prepared for people trying to sell you carpets, chewing gum, or trinkets. Casinos are newly popular, and a more traditional form of entertainment, the *hammam*, or public bath, is widely available in Turkey as well as in Syria.

Outside the tourist areas, few people speak any language except Turkish. This can be a potential problem, so you might want to know a few "catch phrases" before going too far from the main tourist spots. Turkish is a phonetic language: *c* is pronounced *j*, *ç* and *s* are pronounced *ch* or *sh*, *g* is silent but accents the preceding vowel, and the umlauts are pronounced as in German. The country is a mixture of 40 ethnic groups, including Slavs, Europeans, and Asians, and the language reflects that mix.

The area along the coast has ruins of entire ancient civilizations, and most sites are well excavated and enclosed. Take the time to learn about the history of this remarkable region before visiting; background knowledge will undoubtedly enrich an already spectacular trip.

Most cycle tourists enter the country at the Aegean coast between Izmir and Antalya since it's an easy and cheap place to travel, so our route will follow the coast and continue across to Syria from there. You can join or exit the tour at any time. Travel the inland roads at any point you wish—just be ready to downshift as you cross the country's many mountains. Our tour is a terrific ride, a mix of sea and mountain scapes, crowds and isolation, difficult climbs and flats, all through a country rich in natural beauty.

Section 1. From the Greek Border to Izmir

Distance: 565 km direct; 980 km via Istanbul
Terrain: rolling hills
Duration: 5–12 days, depending on the chosen route
Rating: medium difficult

Accommodations

A range of hotels are in all the larger cities and near ruins frequented by Western tourists; in small towns there is ususally just one primitive hotel. Camping areas are near the Dardanelles.

1.1 Greek border to Kesan

Beginning at the Greek border between the Greek town of Feres and Ipsala on the Turkish side, ride 28 km to the large city of Kesan on a wide, hilly road. On the way, you can go into a restaurant and get your first taste of Turkish food as you pass through two small villages. Edirne, one of the nicest towns in Turkey, is over 90 km off our path to the north, near the Bulgarian border—quite a detour.

From Kesan, you have two alternate routes eventually leading to Izmir: Route A leading via Istanbul in the northeast, or Route B for a more direct link hugging the Aegean coast. If you have never been to Istanbul, and have the time, I suggest you take Route A. Choose Route B if you have less time.

Route A. From Kesan to Izmir via Istanbul

A1. Kesan to Istanbul

Distance: 215 km (135 miles)

1. From Kesan, follow the main road east, via Malkara, Inecik to Tekirdag through pleasant country.

2. When you reach Tekirdag, you've covered about 80 km—another 125 to go to Istanbul.

3. Continue along the same road to Silivir. Up to here the road is pleasant enough as you pass through farm areas and small towns.

4. After another 30 km along the road, it becomes gradually busier as you approach the large city, and you face aggressive driving for the last 30 km on a multi-lane road, with trucks and buses spewing black smoke in your face.

Istanbul

However agressive the traffic may seem, few cities can rival Istanbul as an exciting place to visit. There is so much to see and do here that you should consult a regular guide book. Spend some time in this fascinationg city that straddles the Bosphorus between Europe and Asia.

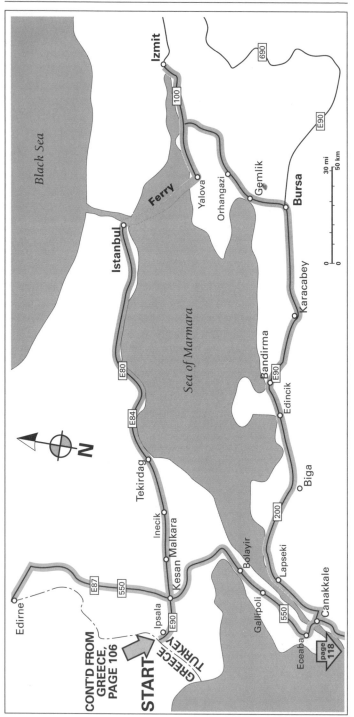

A2. Istanbul to Canakkale

Distance: 400 km (250 miles)

You can't cycle across either of the two bridges across the Bosphorus that connect the European side of Istanbul with the Asian side. It is best to catch a ferry to Yalova from one of the docks at Eminou near the Dolmabahce Palace.

1. From the Yalova dock, follow the signs to Bursa, 55 km away.

2. The road is difficult at first as you travel up through pine-covered mountains, then descend to Orhangazi.

3. From there, the road is wide and basically flat from Umurbey through the city of Bursa. A new road is under construction, which may change this section.

4. Bursa is a large city with a positive atmosphere that becomes more apparent in September during the annual festival. The city is also known for its thermal baths.

5. The road from Bursa to Canakkale is approximately 170 km and is relatively easy. The road begins as a divided highway then quietens as it goes through the green hills to the Sea of Marmara.

6. The section between Biga and Lapseki is more difficult than the flat section leading to Canakkale.

Route B. From Kesan to Canakkale

This route is for those who have decided not to visit Istanbul. Instead, it leads from the Greek border via Kesan straight to a ferry service crossing the Aegean sea to meet up with Route A at Canakkale.

Distance: 260 km

1. From Kesan, do not continue towards Istanbul, but take the road leading southeast (E87 and E90) to Kavak.

2. At Kavak, turn left along the main road leading southwest towards Galipoli. (Gelibolu)

3. The ride along the Dardanelles straight is beautiful, but it was here, between Gallipoli and Canakkale, that the

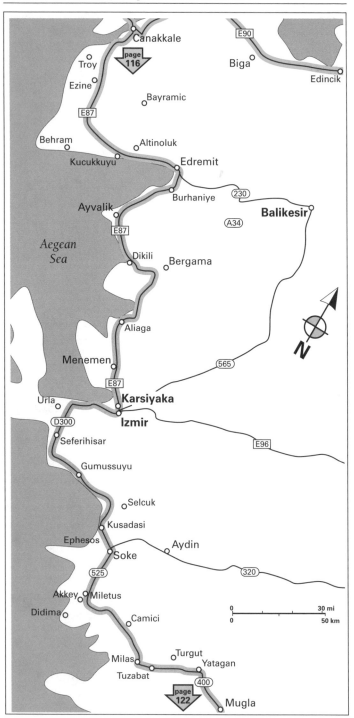

infamous WWI battle in which half a million men perished took place.

4. Continue down the coast to Eceaba and follow the signs for the ferry which will take you across the picturesque strait to Canakkale.

1.3 Canakkale to Izmir

Distance: 340 km (212 miles)

1. At Canakkale, Routes A and B join for the rest of the route down to Izmir.

2. After Canakkale, stay on the coast traveling south on the hilly and scenic road.

3. Follow the signs for Izmir, a whopping 310 km away as you pass several important archeological sites.

Sidetrip to the Trojan ruins

At about 25 km down the road from Canakkale, you will see a sign for Troy (Truva). Make a right turn and take a look at the large wooden horse that greets you as you enter the parking lot. The Trojan ruins are not as extensive as you may have expected, but this is the site of legendary Troy nonetheless, and well worth a short visit. Afterwards, backtrack to the main road and continue south.

Continuation of Route

1. The area continues to be hilly, but it is not very difficult.

2. About 20 km away from the intersection to Bayramic there's a turnoff to the village of Behram (Behramkale). Here you can climb up the road and see the spectacular remains of an acropolis on a cliff by the sea.

3. Continue on the road that hugs the sea through Kucukkuyu and Akcay, where there are thermal baths. This is a beautiful ride.

4. At the intersection just past Edremit, turn right following the signs to Izmir and Bergama. This part of the ride between sea and mountain has a few moderate climbs.

5. The port city of Ayvalik has boats for Lesbos.

6. The ancient site of Pergamum is located right near the modern city of Bergama, and you should allow yourself some time to visit this well-preserved ancient city.

7. Return to the main road and continue south to Aliaga. From here the road is unpleasant—a busy, noisy two-lane affair with trucks and buses.

8. After another 23 km, you reach Menemen, and 11 km from here are the suburbs Koyundere and Ulukent on the outskirts of Izmir.

9. Stay on the road until you see the bay to your right. Soon the road turns into an expressway. At this point, take the side road paralleling the main highway to enter town.

Izmir

Izmir, once known as Smyrna, is a huge city, and biking through it is a long, confusing, and difficult experience. There are plenty of interesting sights, as you will find in any regular guidebook. But I found this city so large and confusing that its beauty, for me at least, was overshadowed. My primary memory of the place is my relief upon leaving the city limits.

Section 2. From Izmir to Antalya

Distance:	575 km (360 miles)
Terrain:	mixture of coast and mountain
Duration:	5–7 days
Rating:	parts are strenous

Accommodations

Towns with complete tourist facilities are Cesme, Selcuk, Kusadasi, Bodrum, Marmaris, Koycegiz, Fethiye, Kas, and Antalya. At least one usually low-end hotel can be found in almost every town. A few rudimentary campgrounds are near tourist areas.

2.1 Izmir to Soke

Distance: 125 km (78 miles)

1. Fortunately, leaving Izmir is not difficult. A new expressway and a smaller road paralleling it both run to Cesme, so ask directions for Cesme and you'll get to the beach road.

2. The road out of Izmir is completely level and passes miles of crowded urban area.

3. About 24 km from the center of Izmir, you see a sign pointing right to Seferihisar on the D300.

4. If you're going to Cesme, about 40 km away, you have a mixture of flats and hills straight along this road. Cesme is a main international port with ferries from Italy, Greece, and the island of Chios. It's one of the nicer tourist centers, and just 5 km outside Cesme on the road to Izmir there is a thermal bath complex at Ilica.

5. The mountainy part of the road from Cesme is between Ilica and the intersection for the road to Karaburun.

6. Pass the seaside town of Urla and, at the intersection for the D300, turn south.

7. The D300 continues essentially flat and quiet until you pass Seferihisar, 20 km from the intersection.

8. The road begins to roll nicely as it passes over cliffs near the sea.

9. Around the town of Erkmev the area is quite flat again.

10. After that you reach Gumussuya and the intersection at Ahmetbeyli about 80 km from Izmir.

11. Continue south and climb again for a couple of km, reach the summit at Ozderl and descend to an intersection for Selcuk and Efes (Ephesos). There turn left.

12. Efes has some of the most spectacular ruins in Turkey. Formerly one of the most important places in Asia Minor, the city is worth the time to stop and see.

13. When you exit Efes, turn left and continue 5 km on the flat road to the D515 to Kusadasi. Kusadasi is the port

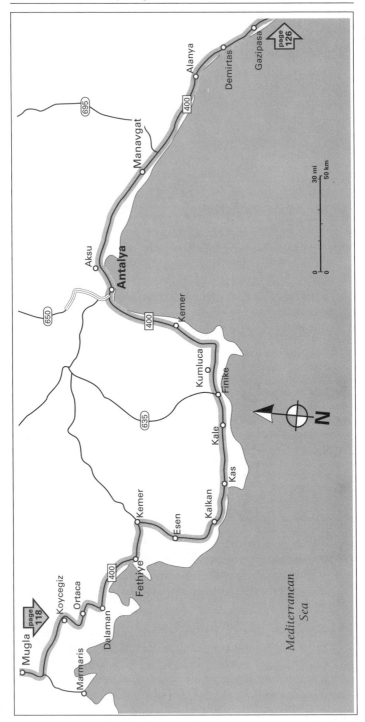

for the island of Samos. The road here is hilly and very pretty near the sea.

14. Two km after the city, you face a steep 3 km climb, with a moderate stretch before you start climbing again until you reach the town of Yayakoy 12 km from Kusadasi.

15. Another 20 km from Kusadasi you arrive at the large town of Soke.

2.2 Soke to Marmaris turnoff

Distance: 161 km (100 miles)

Good cycling and three important cities, Priene, Miletus, and Didima await you on this next part of the tour.

1. From Soke, continue south on the D525, and 2 km later at Yenidogan there's an intersection and a sign for Milas, 81 km.

2. This area, a cotton-growing region, is completely flat for about 24 km and sometimes experiences strong winds from the north and west.

3. Coming near Akkey you see the large Lake Bafa on your left and mountains ahead as the road begins to roll.

4. Turn right at the yellow signs for the cities, and ride up to Priene after 9 km.

5. Miletus is another 9 km, and Didima is at the bottom of the road. After visiting these beautifully preserved cities, backtrack to Akkey and continue east until you return to the D525.

6. After the intersection for Akkey, climb hard for 2 km before proceeding to the towns of Pinarcik and Carnici. Uphill and 1.5 km after Carnici, you must go through a 300 m long dark tunnel. The road is quiet, attractive, and easy to ride to Milas.

7. At the end of the Milas urban area, turn left at the intersection onto the D330 to Mugla, and then begin to climb for 7 km until the town of Tuzabat. The climbs on this road are the most difficult so far. You see lots of bee cultivation and many people selling honey near the road.

8. Continue through Karalti and Eskihisar villages and pass a large strip mine. There's a large industrial plant at the turnoff for Turgut, and soon after is the large city of Yatagan and the end of the road.

9. Turn right on the D550 and follow the signs for Mugla, 26 km, and Antalya, 358 km.

10. Pass the villages of Madenler, Bozarmut, and Bayir and go uphill steadily on a mild grade past Akcaova.

11. Next you pass the town of Mugla and continue on a hilly road for a few km. Climb a steep 2 km until you reach the village of Kizilagac.

12. After 4 km, the road peaks again before descending 7 km on a winding road into the fertile plain below.

13. Continue through Gokova where you see a road to your right for Marmaris, 55 km. This is a popular tourist port since it's connected by a 50 minute hydrofoil to the island of Rhodes, described in Chapter 14.

2.3 Marmaris to Antalya

Distance: 290 km

1. From Marmaris, you face two climbs to get to the main road, the Cetibeli and Sakar Passes. Climb out of town and get on the main road toward Izmir, 284 km away (Yes, we've already been there, so we won't go back all the way).

2. Continue to climb for another 3 km, descend into the village of Getibel, and soon climb again through the pine mountains before descending into the town of Gokova and the intersection to the main coastal road.

3. From the intersection, continue straight toward Fethiye, 106 km, and Antalya.

4. The road is flat through Citlik and uphill for 1 km before Kizilyaka. The road is scenic, with Lake Koycegiz in the distance.

5. Just after Poparlar, exit the main road and enter Koycegiz.

6. Exit Koycegiz by the eastern road.

7. Passing through Sanci, 6 km away, and Ortaca, 17 km away, you reach the town of Fethiye about 57 km from Ortaca. The road is hilly and somewhat rough at this point.

8. You face a several km long winding climb through pine-covered mountains until you reach Dalaman, a large, lively city.

9. From here descend to Gocek and continue up and down for about 20 km from Fethiye.

10. Take the D400 toward Antalya.

11. Passing through Esenkoy, take the coastal route from Kemer down through Esen and Kinik.

12. A few km later there is a sign for Patara, and it is worth visiting this ancient Lycian port, home of St. Nicholas, who somehow became associated with Christmas and climbing down chimneys. Near the Patara ruins is one of Turkey's best beaches.

13. Soon you pass the medium-size town of Yesilokoy, and then there are a couple of hills up to the intersection for the road inland. Near the top we get our first view of the sea since Fethiye.

14. The rest of the way is a nicely curving coastal ride, with the sea ever present below the cliffs, all the way to Kas, a pleasant and frequently visited tourist city.

15. Antalya is another 188 km from Kas. The road from here starts to become more difficult.

16. Right after leaving Kas, climb for several km until the village of Agullu at almost 500 m. The road goes up gradually again until you're on the other side of the mountain. After that, the road continues up and down, with some strenuous climbs along the way through several scenic mountain villages.

17. The road continues down to the plain and goes through Kale to the beach road. The coastal route is attractive and not heavily trafficked. There are pebble beaches along the way to Finike, a town rebuilt after an earthquake.

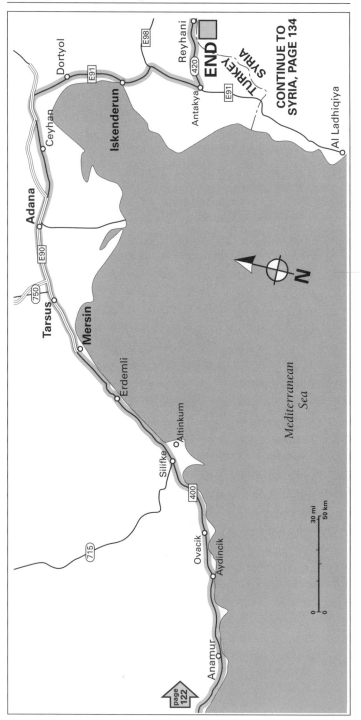

CONTINUE TO
SYRIA, PAGE 134

END

TURKEY
SYRIA

Reyhani

E98

420

Antakya

E91

Al Ladhiqiya

Dortyol

E91

Iskenderun

Ceyhan

Adana

E90

750

Tarsus

Mersin

Erdemli

Altinkum

Silifke

400

Mediterranean
Sea

N

Ovacik

715

Aydincik

30 mi
50 km

0
0

Anamur

page
122

18. From Finike, the road is wide and flat and surrounded by citrus trees.

19. After Kumluca, leave the beach road and take a gentle climb through a pine area for 8–10 km. A bit farther through these rugged mountains there's a turnoff for the Olimpos archeological site and a long, gradual descent through a pine forest.

20. The last 15 km before Kemer are hilly and very pretty. You start getting traffic as you come closer to Kemer. It's worth going the 2 km into the city, as Kemer is one of the nicest towns in the area.

21. The rest of the road to Antalya ranges from easy to moderately difficult. There's a long lit tunnel 25 km from Antalya, and 5 km after the first is an unlit 300 m long tunnel that you must take going uphill. Soon after, you see the city in the distance and begin going through the urban area.

Section 3. From Antalya to Antakya

Distance: 770 km (480 miles)
Terrain: coast and forested mountains
Duration: 5–10 days
Rating: although many sections are flat, overall the tour is difficult

Accommodations

Aim to finish your day at a large city where you have a choice of hotels. In between, there are long stretches of nothing.

3.1 Antalya to Anamur

Distance: 264 km (165 miles)

1. Antalya is not an overly large city, and it's not too difficult to follow the signs out of the city. The road is fairly heavy with traffic on a flat, wide road in the direction of the airport.

2. After the airport, you pass a town called Aksu. Follow the signs for Mersin, about 480 km from Antalya.

3. The signs for the Belek tourism center will take you to Manavgat a few km away.

4. There's a turnoff to Side, 2 km away, if you want to take the short ride to visit this relaxed beach city, which has extensive ruins right next to the sea.

5. About 10 km past Manavgat, there's a turnoff for the D693 which takes you through the mountains to Konya. After that turnoff the road remains flat, but it gradually becomes more scenic as you head toward the beach.

6. About 25 km outside of Alanya, you begin passing hotel areas full of Russian tourists, and in Alanya itself you will find many interesting sights, including a large walled castle on the hill near the sea. There is a ferry from the small port to Northern Cyprus a few times a week. Cyprus is covered in Chapter 11.

7. The road continues flat along the sandy beach as you pass the new tourist developments awaiting the anticipated expansion of the tourist industry.

8. After the turnoff to Demirtas, the road begins to roll gently and continues along the sea. From here you proceed to Gazipasa, and the road becomes more and more interesting as you go east.

9. It's 81 km to Anamur, on a difficult road with three major climbs but hardly any traffic. The area is uninhabited, and the sea is far below you as you ride through this beautiful area.

10. The gradual and winding descent starts about 53 km from Anamur. It's about an 8 km climb (to about 350 m) 37 km from Anamur. Continue on the winding road to the city, which is by no means a pretty place.

3.2 Anamur to Mersin

Distance: 253 km (158 miles)

1. From Anamur, go straight on to Bozyazi, 11 km away.

2. Just after the sign for Aydincik, 29 km, you begin to go uphill for 1 km through a farm area. The road continues along the beach, with a couple of short climbs before the road descends at about 10 km from Aydincik. There's another 1 km climb, then you come into a village and later a populated farm area.

3. Outside Aydincik there's a sign for Silifke, 82 km, and Mersin, 167 km, and at the latter sign you climb another scenic hill for 7 km to 300 m before descending.

4. About 30 km away from Aydincik is the beach community of Ovacik. Shortly after is a hill that climbs to 250 m.

5. When you start coming down you see Tasucu, which has ferry and hydrofoil service to and from Northern Cyprus (see Chapter 11).

6. The ride to Silifke, 11 km, is short and fast. Leaving town, you cross a river and follow the signs for Erdemil, 46 km and Mersin, 83 km. The earth is a rich brown and the surrounding hills rocky. Along the way you spot a castle sitting on a small island just off the coast.

7. Soon you reach the town of Kizkalesi, which has some interesting ruins and a few other tourist attractions. Next you come to Erdemli and continue on to Mersin, 35 km, a fairly modern port city.

3.3 Mersin to Antakya

Distance: 252 km (157 miles)

1. Follow the same road straight through the city, following the signs for Ankara and Adana. You won't be missing anything if you decide to take a bus past Adana; the road is somewhat monotonous and busy.

2. If you decide to ride, Tarsus is almost 30 km away, and a couple of km later is the turnoff for Ankara. Adana is

another 40 km away. There's a service road for a little while, but then it's the shoulder of a busy road the rest of the way. After Adana the road becomes quieter.

3. Take the turnoff for Misis (Yakapinar) to Ceyhan.

4. In Ceyhan, ask directions for the road to Yumurtalik.

5. About 15 km out of town on the quiet road, you will see a sign for Dortyol. This is an up and down road that hugs the coast for a short while. After the initial 10–15 km, the road becomes fairly flat.

6. After another 15–20 km you cross the railroad track and hit the main road to Antakya. This is a busy road with a shoulder that's even more bumpy.

7. You have to exit to get into Dortyol, and 2 km later you come to Payas, a heavily industrialized area. These seaside towns are dominated by heavy industry, not tourism, and as we roll into Iskenderun, it will be our last view of the sea for a while.

8. Follow the two-lane highway to Antakya and soon the road becomes hilly.

9. Make the steep climb into the village of Sarimazi, descend briefly, then climb for another 7 km until you reach the Belen Pass at 740 m. It's a terrific ride down from here until the end of the intersection for the D825.

10. Now stay on the right toward Antakya, 30 km away. The road is flat, straight, and well trafficked. The rest of the road to the border is rolling hills.

11. Follow the blue signs for Reyhani and Cilvegozu, 48 km, and the yellow signs for Halep, 105 km. There are military installations around, so hide your camera.

12. About 20 km from Antakya, pass the market village of Vemirkotru and cross a river. Then climb a 2 km hill only 10 km from the border to reach Reyhani.

13. Just before the border, merge into a larger road and see the line of tractor-trailers waiting for border formalities.

If you're continuing, get your passport stamped and ride across the long stretch of no-man's-land to the Syrian checkpoint. This is where our tour of Syria and Lebanon picks up—see Chapter 8.

Chapter 8
Syria and
Lebanon

Syria and Lebanon are perhaps better known for political turmoil than for cycling, but both countries offer the intrepid traveler a unique experience. As of this writing, the U.S. State Department forbids American nationals from traveling to Lebanon, but that ban may be lifted in the near future. The Syrian army now occupies Lebanon, and the two countries are merging politically, to the dismay of some Lebanese. You must have a visa prior to entering these countries, which you can obtain at your local Syrian consulate. There's a fee of about $20, and you need to fill out a form and provide two pictures. You can usually obtain visas in Syrian consulates abroad within a day. Currently, if you have an Israeli stamp in your passport, you will be denied a visa.

Transcription of Arabic names is a perpetual problem since there is no universally accepted standard. A newspaper editor once counted fifteen different ways in which newspapers spelled Colonel Qaddafi's name. Arabic

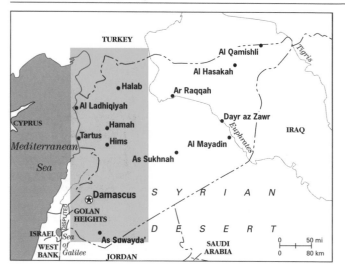

is difficult for most English speakers to pronounce because it contains sounds from the throat. However, locals really enjoy it if you try to say a couple of Arabic words, so make an attempt to learn the easy ones. Almost everyone you meet will try to help you find your way around, but not all directions are reliable, so ask frequently about the roads. Policemen are usually terrible sources of information.

Syria, because of the increased political and economic stability of recent years, is a very accessible place for the tourist. You face less of a language problem than in Turkey since more people speak English here. Even in the small villages they will dig out a person to translate for you. The main roads are generally of good quality and smoother than in Turkey. This is a physically beautiful area, and with the proper attitude of respect for the people and their culture, you will have the time of your life.

We will take the coastal road from Turkey into Syria and Lebanon, but other overland routes exist from southern Turkey and Jordan. The only regular ferry service is the one between Junyeh north of Beirut and Cyprus. A number of airlines have international flights into Beirut, Damascus, and Aleppo.

Syria is one of the least expensive countries on our tour. You will most likely spend about as much here as you would in Turkey. The many open-air markets and the wonderful cuisine are two of this cultures' finer specialties, so enjoy bargaining and sampling new foods.

The tourism industry has not yet arrived, but it probably will. Recently a couple of camping grounds have sprung up. This entire area, including Iraq, is loaded with incredible archeological sites that are unfortunately not well maintained.

Lebanon has a history of tolerance and decadence; rich Europeans and Arabs used to come here on holiday years ago to ski and to swim. Time and war have transformed the area a great deal, but much remains the same. However, at the moment, South Lebanon is in an active state of war and should be avoided. If you do have the opportunity to visit, be sure to read about this country and its history before you arrive. The tourist offices are next to useless.

As for maps, a reasonably detailed map is the Hildebrand Travel Map of Syria, Lebanon, and Jordan—although at a scale of 1:1,250,000, at least it's available in the United States and Europe, while it may be hard to find anything better once you are there. Cartographia's map of Syria at 1:1,000,000 is more detailed. For Lebanon, there are some reasonable maps published by the National Council of Tourism, and a 1:200,000 map by Bartholomew, and Geoprojects publishes maps of both countries.

Summary of the Route

Our route starts in the northern part of Syria at the border with Turkey, linking up with the tour described in Chapter 7. It continues down to Jordan via Damascus, with an optional detour through Lebanon.

After having your passport stamped at the border, you can proceed unhassled into the country. If a guard asks you for money, there is no reason to give it to him. You will notice many trucks waiting at the border; they tend to travel in convoys. If you begin seeing a convoy passing you, it's a good idea to get off the road for a break.

You notice an immediate physical difference as soon as you enter the country as the surrounding hills change from lush green to rocky brown. Syria appears to be a flat, wide plain, but as you ride you notice the gradual rising and falling of the road.

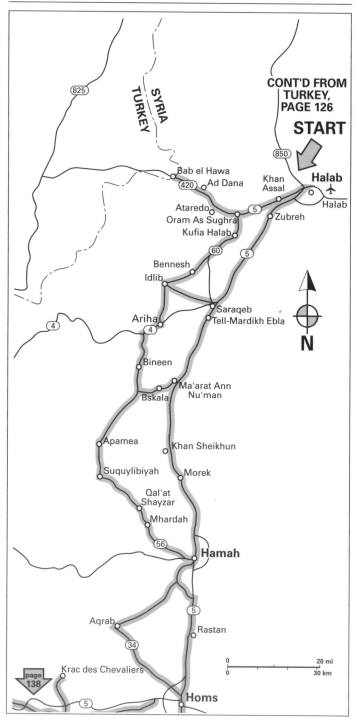

Section 1. From the Turkish Border to Hamah

Distance: 225 km (140 miles) direct
Terrain: plateau farm land
Duration: 2–3 days
Rating: moderate

Accommodations

There are hotels in Aleppo, Idlib, and Hamah. In most villages, someone will happily put you up.

1.1 Turkish border to Idlib

Distance: 120 km (75 miles)

1. From the border, follow the gently climbing road for 7 km until you come to an intersection for Bab-el-Hawa.

2. Follow the sign for Aleppo, which in Arabic is called Halab, and you see the village of Ad Dana off the road. Continue down this road, which is nice and quiet with very few cars.

3. A bit after Ad Dana, the road begins to descend as you pass Ataredo and come to an intersection with signs written only in Arabic. There are old blue tombs across the road.

4. Turn left in the direction of Halab, and continue on the road as it passes by a few villages. Slowly, the traffic increases as you ride toward the city.

5. Aleppo (Halab) is one of Syria's most interesting cities. Like the city of Jericho, Aleppo bills itself as the world's oldest continuously inhabited city. It has been a center of trade for 4,000 years. Visit the Citadel, the mosques, the museum, and the souk, and stroll through the bustling, old city.

6. The main road, which we will be taking part of the way, traverses the country through Damascus into Jordan. This Damascus road, often called *tarik-al-Sham* (Sham is the local name for Damascus), is reliable but not as scenic as the smaller roads, so we will occasionally take these for some variety. When leaving Aleppo, get on the

main road to Damascus and backtrack to the turnoff
with the tombs before riding straight to Idlib.

7. The road rolls along gently as you cycle through this
beautiful, peaceful area.

8. The first village you pass on your left is Sheikh Ali, then
after a slight hill you go through Kufia Halab, a typical
stone village. The signs that mark these small places, if
they exist at all, are usually only in Arabic.

9. Soon you reach the villages of Kufr Nuran, Shalah, and
Taftanaz. You need to get off the road slightly to go into
these settlements.

10. A sign directs you straight to Latakia.

11. The next village is Taaoum, and from here you continue
up and down through the large town of Bennesh.

12. In a short while you're in one of the country's larger
cities, Idlib. There is not much to see in Idlib besides the
museum, but it's a friendly town.

1.2 Idlib to Tell-Mardikh-Ebla

Distance: 25 km (15 miles)

1. Instead of following the road straight through the city
toward Ariha, ask for the road to Sarageb on the
Damascus Road, and you will be directed to a wide
road with very little traffic.

2. The road passes Sarmeen, a sleepy old town. People will
come up to you, ask you where you're from, and direct
you to the proper road. This area is populated by family
farms cultivating a variety of produce on their own land.

3. You arrive at a main road to Latakia before coming to
the Damascus Road. The town of Sarageb is just off the
road as you take the turn onto the Damascus Road. The
road is not busy at this point and has a shoulder.

4. Be alert here for signs leading to Tell-Mardikh-Ebla Ebla
for short), 4–5 km from the turnoff. Or ask someone to
point you toward Ebla, and you will be directed to a
small road that goes to this historical site.

5. Ebla is significant for its wonderful ruins of a city that
    was destroyed in 2250 BC, which was in its time the
    most developed in the region. The citizens had their
    own writing system and inscribed over 17,000 clay
    tablets. If you're not interested in these ruins, preferring
    to take the small roads through more villages, you can
    continue from Idlib to Ariha and meet up with us
    farther south.

1.3 Tell-Mardikh-Ebla to Hamah

Distance: 80 km (50 miles) direct

1. From Ebla's historic site, return to the main road, which
    is comfortable as long as the convoy of trucks from
    Turkey is not passing. It's the same gently rising and
    falling road that we find all over Syria, and the rich
    rocky earth that surrounds it is planted with vegetables,
    olive trees, pistachios, and fruits.

2. The next town is Khan al-Sabel, then Bineen, and soon
    after, Ma'arat an-Nu'man.

3. Go through Ma'arat an-Nu'man, and either return to the
    smooth, safe main road and continue all the way to
    Hamah, or take the smaller quiet road that rolls through
    one village after another. The main road straight to
    Hamah is about 65 km, while along the smaller road
    through Suquylibiyah it is about 100 km.

4. If you opt for the small road, in Ma'arat-an-Nu'man ask
    for the road to Kufr Nubbul, and you will be directed to
    a small road through the town which passes Bskala. It's
    a hilly road from the start.

5. At the end of town there's a turnoff to al-Qeilbiyeh,
    about 30 km away. Thereafter, the road becomes busy in
    places.

6. From Suquylibiyah, continue toward Hamah on a
    sometimes narrow and busy road. There are many
    places to stop along the way, and the many people you
    meet will treat you to tea and conversation.

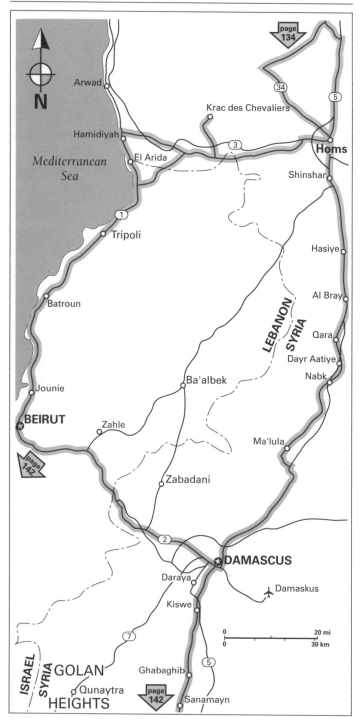

N

Arwad

Krac des Chevaliers

page 134

34

5

Hamidiyah

El Arida

3

Homs

Mediterranean Sea

Shinshar

1

Tripoli

Hasiye

Al Bray

Batroun

Qara

LEBANON

SYRIA

Dayr Aatiye

Nabk

Jounie

Ba'albek

BEIRUT

Zahle

Ma'lula

page 142

Zabadani

2

DAMASCUS

Daraya

Damaskus

Kiswe

0   20 mi
0   30 km

7

ISRAEL

SYRIA

GOLAN

Ghabaghib

5

Qunaytra

page 142

HEIGHTS

Sanamayn

7. At Mhardah, where there's a castle on a hill, you pass a couple of roundabouts and may need to ask for the road to Hamah.

8. Hamah is another ancient city, lively and interesting to tour. To many, the city is known for a violent struggle in the early 1980s, but you will find no scars of this era. If instead you opted for the main road from Ma'arat an-Nu'man straight to Hamah, you will find this road is also nice and certainly not as difficult, although it still has some moderate climbs.

Section 2. From Hamah to Der'a

Distance: 305 km (190 miles)
Terrain: mountain desert
Duration: 2–4 days
Rating: the section between Homs and Damascus is
                unpleasant and difficult; the rest is moderate

Accommodations

Hotels are in the larger cities. Elsewhere, you'll find the local people hospitable.

2.1 Hamah to Homs

Distance: 65 km (40 miles) direct

1. From the center of Hamah, where there is a large clock, continue southwest and begin asking people for the road to Kufr Bahem and Aqrab.

2. When you reach a bus station, go up a small hill and see a sign announcing the road to Aqrab, 33 km away.

3. The road passes a military airfield and an industrial area, then becomes more scenic and hilly. The road surface is not great.

4. At Kufr Bahem there's a fork; if you take the left side you will return to the highway on an uninteresting road, but if you continue right for about 3 km you will come to a village and see the road back to the main highway. This road is also much farther than the

straight road to our next main town, Homs, so only take the quiet road for a short while before returning to the main highway at al-Rastan (referred to simply as Rastan on our map).

5. The highway, which looks straight and flat on maps, is actually quite hilly, with several 100 m and 200 m variations in altitude.

6. A couple of km from the town there's a bypass for Damascus and a service road that exits the main highway. The road continues to the town center. If you prefer, you can continue to Aqrab and take the road through Taldau.

7. Homs is another vibrant Arab city with a couple of ancient churches to visit. From here there is a new 200 km road to Tadmor/Palmyra, an ancient city that rises out of the desert. I have not yet ridden out here, but those who have describe it as a relatively easy ride through some wonderful villages.

Optional Tour from Homs into Lebanon

We also have from here an optional trip through Lebanon, stopping first in Tripoli, then continuing to Beirut and returning to Syria by way of Damascus, where this route links up with the Syrian tour. Lebanon is a lovely country, and if the situation in the country becomes more stable, I would highly recommend at least the first part of this route. If you choose not to travel through Lebanon, continue straight to Damascus from Homs, as described in Section 2.4.

A. Homs to Tripoli

Distance: 90 km (56 miles)

1. From Homs, take the main road to Tartus, and about 10 km later you see a quieter side road.

2. You see the mountains of Lebanon on your left as you pass, and the road is barren and empty.

3. Go through Talkalakh, where you can ride up and see Krac des Chevaliers.

4. After 10 km you reach the main road and another road to Dabusyeh, which was once an international crossing, but no longer.

5. Continue to Hamidiyah on the coast, then cross the border at El Arida.

6. From here, it's about 20 km to Tripoli (Tarablos), which is on a flat coastal road. It's a pretty ride down to the capital, passing the port of Junie, which has a ferry service to Cyprus (see Chapter 11).

B. Tripoli via Beirut to Damascus

Distance: 200 km (137 miles)

1. From Tripoli, travel south via the coastal main road for about 90 km, passing through Amchit, Byblos and Jounie.

2. From Beirut, take the main road east, through the town known as Cola (there used to be a bottling plant there) and climb up the mountain toward Zahle.

3. At the junction about 10 km before Zahle, fork right toward Damascus via Chtaura and Masnaa.

4. The road to Damascus is quite heavily trafficked but wide. It winds up through Barlayas and continues to climb to the border. After that point, your ride is relatively easy, but the traffic increases as you near the Syrian capital.

2.4 Homs to Damascus

Distance: 140 km (87 miles)

If you decide not to take the road through Lebanon, the main highway is basically the only road to Damascus from Homs, and it is difficult.

1. There are signs from Homs to the main road, which is two lanes with a shoulder that is sometimes paved and sometimes dirt.

2. On the first part of the road, there is a constant climb until you reach 600 m near Shamsien to al-Qusair.

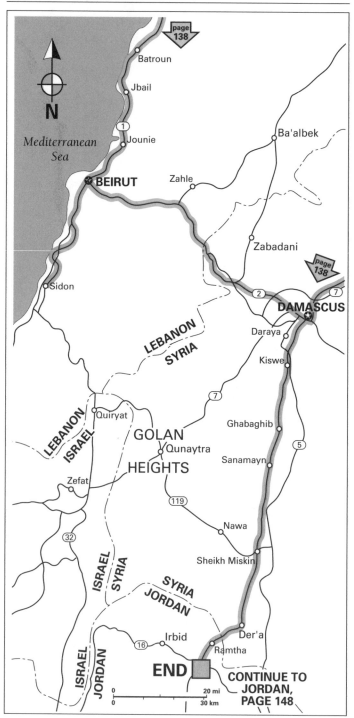

3. You can spot some industry near the road, but there's almost no farming in this dry area. Take a left into Hasiye and come out the other side. The road continues up and down, but around Hasiye you begin to feel the grade more. A long, gradual climb starts at the 115 km mark.

4. The road remains light with traffic as you take another climb at Al Bray and exit onto the old highway right next to the main road. The climate here is hot and dry.

5. The road continues to climb as a sign welcomes you to Dayr Aatiye.

6. A bit after the 90 km mark, you see a large statue of President Assad on a hill, and you enter Nabk on the local road. The old road goes in and out of the main highway, and at the 65 km mark we reach our peak height of about 1,350 m.

7. The stretch after Nabk on the local road is quiet and empty. The road now descends quickly through the arid, dusty terrain. You begin seeing light industry nearby, then suddenly you come upon the highrises of a city surrounded by barren mountains. You pass Ma'lula, a pleasant mountain town that is famous for the fact that the inhabitants still speak the language that was spoken at the time of Christ.

Damascus

Damascus makes a lot of noise, but it's not difficult to navigate. It seems hard to believe when you're surrounded by the indigence and disorder of the city, but Damascus, along with Cairo and Baghdad, was a main center for knowledge and learning in the Islamic world after the Omayyad Dynasty (661–750 AD) made Damascus its capital. The museum is really wonderful, as is walking around the streets.

2.5. Damascus to Der'a

Distance: 100 km (62 miles)

1. Leave Damascus on the main highway going south, and a bit later there are signs for Beirut and for Der'a and Amman, Jordan.

2. About 10 km from the center of Damascus, you come to a sign directing you to the expressway. Don't take that route, but continue down the old road instead.

3. There's a 1 km climb, then you go over the expressway, and you can see where the two roads are going south.

4. Soon after you continue through Kiswe, where there's an unmarked roundabout. The road surface is not great and the surrounding area is barren.

5. There's a brief climb before the turnoff to Zreiqiyeh, about 30 km from Damascus.

6. Continue through Sanamayn, an industrial town, and the road becomes quiet. There's something beautiful about the bare scenery and dusty villages.

7. The rest of the road through Sheikh Miskin and into Der'a is a relatively flat and comfortable ride.

8. Along the way, you can take the turnoff into the dry city of Izraa, which has a couple of early Christian churches.

2.7 Der'a to the Jordanian Border

Distance: 16 km (10 miles)

1. As you leave Der'a, you begin to encounter truck traffic from the main road. The drivers are not kind to cyclists.

2. Nearby there is a refugee camp for those who used to live in the Golan Heights. Continue through a populated area to the border complex.

If you plan to continue into Jordan, cross the Syrian border post and go downhill for a couple of km to reach the Jordanian immigration offices. The route description continues from here in Chapter 9.

Chapter 9
Jordan

A small and friendly country to visit, Jordan is nonetheless a challenging cycling experience. The northwest part of the country is where the majority of the population lives, and the rest of the land is desert. This populated area is very hilly. Once you leave the population center between Amman and Irbid, expect to enjoy long empty rides. The country is not large, and you can ride down the length of it in three days if you want to. Jordan does not have many roads, but the surfaces are in good condition.

As of this writing, negotiations are under way with Israel to open other roads between the two countries. In the future perhaps, there will be more entry and exit points to the country. Our route takes the route from Syria on the main road between the two countries. Another road goes into Saudi Arabia, but Saudi Arabia does not permit tourists unless they have business in their country. A new road opened in 1994 at Aqaba, which passes through the Israeli resort of Elat to the Egyptian town of Taba. As far as air travel is concerned, the Amman airport has international flights from around the world.

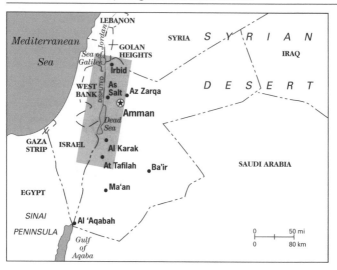

Jordan used to be fairly expensive until the 1980s, but now it is only slightly more expensive than Syria. A hotel will cost as little as $6 a night, and a meal in the many Arab fast food places—hummus, falafil—costs less than $1. There are no campgrounds here, but people living away from the populated areas are happy to offer a place to stay. It is better to obtain a visa before arriving in the country, but the authorities will stamp a visa in your passport upon arrival. Visas cost about $20 and are available to just about every nationality.

The same Hildebrands Travel Map at scale 1:1,250,000 we used for Syria and Lebanon will probably serve you adequately on this route. Much more detailed are the Bartholomew map of Israel and Jordan at 1:250,000 (though it does not cover all of Jordan) and the Geoproject Jordan map at 1:730,000.

From the Syrian Border to the Israel Border

Distance: 150–400 km (93—250 miles)
Terrain: rugged mountains
Duration: 2–5 days
Rating: strenuous

Accommodations

Only main cities have hotels.

1. Syrian Border to Amman

Distance: 85 km

1. Starting at the entry point from Syria, continue straight toward the mid-size town of Ramtha.

2. Follow the signs on the hilly road through town directing you to the road to Amman, 85 km away.

3. A few km later is a crossroads for the highway to Irbid, Mafraq, and the Iraqi border, and a few km after that is another crossroads. Keep riding on the gradually rising road.

4. At the 56 km mark, just after the turnoff for Jerash, is a 900 m climb in which the last couple of km are steep. This climb is followed by a 7% descent.

5. Go into Jerash, one of Jordan's nicest cities, and see the historic sites, which include extensive Roman ruins. Then get back onto the main highway via the connecting road south of the city.

6. At the 40 km mark, drop to less than 250 m before beginning to climb 4–5 km to 450 m. The road is getting a bit busier and more difficult at this point.

7. Another 3–4 km climb takes us up to 600 m at the 32 km mark.

8. After the Bedawi refugee camp, climb again for about 7 km until you reach a roundabout at Suweleh.

9. Turn left, climb for another 0.5 km, and then follow the sign to Amman. The elevation here is about 1000 m, and the road is quite busy.

10. Continue straight into town, following the signs for the city center and descending into the city. Amman has a Roman theater in the middle of town, but not much more of outstanding beauty. It also has several steep, long hills, and getting around the city involves a bit of pushing. You don't see other cyclists.

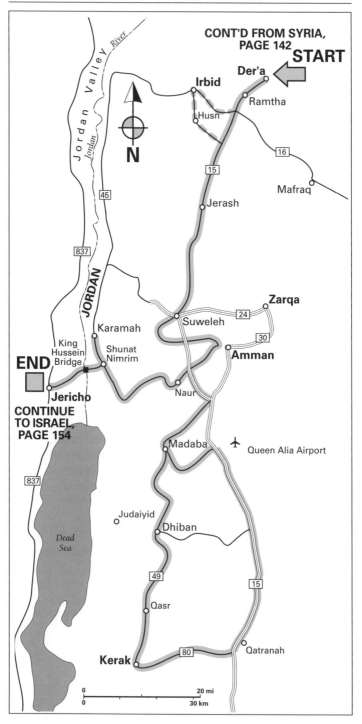

CONT'D FROM SYRIA,
PAGE 142

START

Der'a

Irbid

Ramtha

Husn

Jordan Valley River

Jordan

N

15

16

Jerash

Mafraq

45

837

JORDAN

Zarqa

24

Suweleh

30

Karamah

King
Hussein
Bridge

Shunat
Nimrim

Amman

END

Naur

Jericho

CONTINUE
TO ISRAEL,
PAGE 154

Madaba

Queen Alia Airport

837

Judaiyid

Dhiban

*Dead
Sea*

49

15

Qasr

80

Qatranah

Kerak

0   20 mi
0   30 km

2. Round Trip from Amman

Distance: 230 km (143 miles)

From Amman, you can visit some important historical sites.

1. Take the road to the airport from Amman and follow the signs for Madaba.

2. Come to Judaiyid and soon after an intersection where the main road continues down to Aqaba, 310 km away, or goes to Madaba.

3. The smaller road to Madaba is hilly and difficult, but Madaba is a nice city with famous mosaics of the map of ancient Palestine.

4. The route also has some beautiful vistas along the way. Either continue down the old King's Highway to Kerak or return to the main highway by another hilly road near the airport.

5. After the airport, the main road becomes quieter. It looks like an expressway, but it has a wide shoulder.

6. Just after the sign for Aqaba (290 km), there's a 2–3 km hill through the bare countryside.

7. Many km of lonely biking later, you arrive at Qatranah, the first real town along this road.

8. The road continues straight to Petra if you decide to visit this city, but otherwise take the turn to Karak, 40 km away, about 5 km south of Qatranah.

9. The road west begins to climb right away for about 5 km through the dark barren hills.

10. Just before Kerak, there's a village off the side of the road at the intersection for the King's Highway. Soon the famous castle comes into view. From here, simply return to Amman the way you came.

3. Amman to the Israeli Border

Distance: 65 km (40 miles)

The route from Amman to Israel is via the King Hussein Bridge, about 65 km from downtown Amman. There are a couple of ways to find this road, but probably the easiest way is via the Jabal district of Amman.

1. After climbing from the center, come to the 7th circle and face the road going down to the airport or up to Irbid.

2. Take the airport road for about 4 km until you see a sign for the Dead Sea.

3. Turn right, and you'll see signs for Naur and Marj al-Hammam. You'll be about 900 m above the sea.

4. Continue along the road to Naur, where there are hot springs; from there, pick up the old highway to the Dead Sea.

5. The road is mainly downhill from here on, as the Dead Sea, just south of the bridge, is 400 m below sea level.

6. The old road eventually turns into a dirt road and feeds into the nice new road. It now has little traffic, but perhaps in the future if borders open this will change.

7. At the 33 km mark you hit sea level as the road continues to descend.

8. Instead of following the road to the Dead Sea, continue to your right at the fork just after the sea level mark.

9. Shortly after the turnoff, you come to a green valley and look over a wide expanse of cultivated land, which seems odd after so many miles of rugged desert.

10. No sign directs you to Israel, but soon you will see signs for Shunat Nimrim and the King Hussein Bridge.

11. From here there is another road north through the valley to Karamah. The most significant feature of this entire valley is its oppressive summer heat. For this reason, winter is an ideal time for visiting.

As of the time of writing, you will need a permit from the Interior Ministry in Amman in order to cross the border into Israel. Unfortunately, Israel currently has a rule that prohibits anyone from bringing a bicycle over the border. Be sure to ask at your Jordanian and Israeli consulates about this rule so you will be prepared. The Israel tour is described in Chapter 10.

Chapter 10
Israel

Israel is a cultural mix of Jews from Europe and Russia, Arabic or Asian Jews, and Palestinians, so it is half a European country and half a Middle Eastern country in spirit. Both Jews and Palestinians have an exceptionally high level of education, and if the country can harmonize its religious and social diversity, it will be a wonderful place.

Despite its image, Israel is a safe area for tourists. When traveling through the West Bank and Gaza you will get much better treatment from the Palestinians if you wear conservative dress and perhaps the kefeyah head dress.

Bicycle touring here can be lots of fun. It is a small country: a strong cyclist can easily ride the length of the country on the coast, from the Lebanese to the Egyptian borders, in a day. That area is a coastal plain that becomes drier the farther you move south. A strong mountain range runs down the country's interior from Mt. Carmel overlooking the port at Haifa down to the Negev Desert. Galilee and the entire West Bank is mountainous and difficult to ride, with its towns, including the Jerusalem area, at high altitudes. It often snows here in winter.

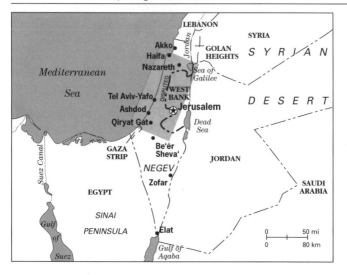

Be sure to contact the Israeli consulate or tourist office back home to ask for up-to-date information on border crossings before coming here. The borders at Elat to Egypt at Rafah and Jordan at Aqaba are open, but the ride to Elat and then around the Sinai is long and empty. At this moment, these are the only borders you can cross by bicycle, but currently Jordan and Israel are negotiating another open border.

Israel has international flights to the airport at Tel Aviv and some direct flights to Elat. Shop around, and you will usually be able to get bargain fares. The main port at Haifa has ferry service from Cyprus, Pireaus, Crete, Rhodes, Alexandria, and Brindisi. Muslims respect Friday afternoon as their holy day, Jews respect Saturday, and Christians keep Sunday. Friday noon to Saturday sundown is not a good time to arrive in the country.

Israel is a moderately expensive country, but it is possible to find hotels in Jerusalem for under $10 a night and meals for $5. The West Bank and Gaza are cheaper areas, while the coast tends to be more expensive. In general, the Arab areas are cheaper than Israeli ones. Cycling is not a popular sport here, so you will find few good bicycle shops. In the Gaza many people use clunkers, while in Israel you will meet the occasional person, often an American, out for a training ride on a racing bike. The country has a handful of campgrounds on the coast and near the Sea of Galilee, but I've seen many people camp on their own in isolated areas.

Just about any road here is good for cycling. Traffic around the cities is heavy, but most country roads are nice for riding. Our tour starts at Jericho near the Dead Sea and swings around the country. If you want to stick to easy rides, stay west, but much of that area is not as interesting to ride as the hillier roads.

Good maps are available locally, such as Bayak's 1:250,000 scale map published by Steimatsky's. A reasonably good map also available abroad is the Israel Touring Map at scale 1:400,000, which is published by the IGTO, the national tourist office. Bartholomew and Freytag & Berndt publish good maps at scales 1:250,000 and 1:400,000 respectively.

Round Trip to Gaza

Distance: 420 km (260 miles)
Terrain: hilly east, flat west
Duration: 3–7 days
Rating: from easy to very difficult

Accommodations

There is so much to see here that many people spend a lot of time sightseeing. All Israeli tourist areas have complete facilities including many hotels, and the larger Palestinien cities are now developing this business. There are a few camping areas and several hostels along the coast.

1. Jericho to Jerusalem

Distance: 40 km (25 miles)

Jericho, called Areha in Arabic, has an historical *tel* and an impressive nearby monastery cut into the rock mountain. An area rich with agriculture, it harvests enormous grapefruits, radishes, and other produce that can only grow in this sub–sea level natural greenhouse.

1. Follow the main road to Jerusalem, first south for a few miles, then east. In summer it's like cycling in a sauna, so bring plenty of water.

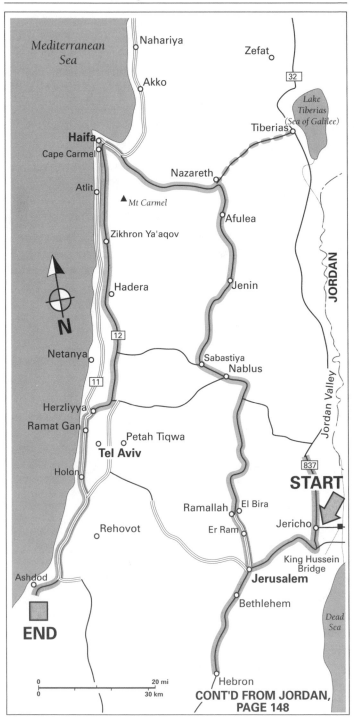

Mediterranean Sea

Nahariya

Zefat

32

Akko

Lake Tiberias (Sea of Galilee)

Haifa

Tiberias

Cape Carmel

Nazareth

Atlit

▲ *Mt Carmel*

Afulea

Zikhron Ya'aqov

N

Hadera

Jenin

12

Netanya

Sabastiya

11

Nablus

Herzliyya

Ramat Gan

Petah Tiqwa

Tel Aviv

Holon

START

Ramallah

El Bira

Rehovot

Er Ram

Jericho

King Hussein Bridge

Ashdod

837

Jerusalem

END

Bethlehem

Dead Sea

JORDAN

Jordan Valley

0   20 mi
0   30 km

Hebron

CONT'D FROM JORDAN, PAGE 148

2. It's mainly uphill to Jerusalem. A long and difficult climb, it starts shortly after you arrive at the crossroads for Jerusalem and the Dead Sea and ends at the outskirts of the greater Jerusalem area.

3. Turn right at the crossroads, and after Nabi Musa the climbing starts. There isn't much on this road except a sea level marker, some goats, and roads leading to military areas.

4. As you're climbing, you pass the settlement of Maale Adummim on your left. Like all West Bank settlements, it resembles a fortress more than it does a residential community.

5. About 10 km from Jerusalem, called al-Qud in Arabic and Yerushalayim in Hebrew, you pass the Arab towns of Abu Dis and Silwan before coming to the walls of the old city.

Jerusalem

Most budget travelers stay in hostels in the Old City; all parts of the modern city have more expexsive hotels. Visit the sights: the Church of the Holy Sepulchre, the Wailing Wall, the Dome of the Rock, the Mount of Olives, the Crusader walls, the Mea Shearim Orthodox district, the Yad VaShem Holocaust memorial, the Arab *souk*, or market.

Sidetrip to Bethlehem

Distance: 12 km each way

From Jerusalem, it is a short distance to Bethlehem on a winding, up-and-down road that passes a couple of Jewish settlements and a Palestinian refugee camp. The road down to Hebron, called Khalil in Arabic, is also hilly and difficult, winding through the barren brown hills.

2. Jerusalem to Haifa via Nazareth

Distance: 195 km (121 miles)

1. When you're ready to leave Jerusalem, go through the Arab area past Sheikh Jarrah and take the fairly busy road north to Ramallah through a populated area. It's a

short ride but not difficult. The Palestinians in this region can be hostile to those wearing skimpy clothes, which in their minds they associate with Israelis, so you might want to decorate your head with a kefeyah head dress—or keep it handy on top of your handlebar bag to don when you need it.

2. Shortly you reach Ramallah, a lively and pleasant town.

3. From here, continue north through the hills to Nablus. It's not far, 45 km, but the road is winding, slightly narrow in some places, and has a tight descent about 15 km from Ramallah. Considering that this is the main road through the West Bank, it isn't that heavily trafficked.

4. Continue straight through the city, but don't pass up visiting the central market area.

5. From here, continue on the main road to the village of Deir Sharaf, then turn right and go through the mountains by following the sign for Jenin, 33 km from the turnoff. This is a difficult road that goes through Burqa.

6. These beautiful roads go up and down the hills and pass villages where life seems to have changed little since the time of Christ.

7. You reach Jenin, another pleasant city, and from here continue north to Afulea, 17 km on an easier road.

8. Now cross over into Israel proper and continue another 10 km to Nazareth on the up-and-down road. Nazareth is a city on hills, and riding around is difficult.

From here you can continue down to the Sea of Galilee at Tiberias, but we will proceed to the coast and follow the signs to Haifa. There's a junction at Hiryat Ata, and after that the traffic picks up as you see the green plain in front of you. Haifa is the only integrated city in the country: Arabs and Jews live and work side by side.

3. Haifa to Tel Aviv and Gaza

Distances: 95 km and 175 km (59 and 109 miles), respectively

1.   From Haifa, head south on the old road to Tel Aviv, which starts out as a highway around the coast but then has a marked turnoff to the old road via En Hod. This is an easy road with a couple of camping areas right on the beach.

2.   Once you hit Netanya, you enter a large urban area through Tel Aviv, which is a very unattractive city. It's a heavily populated area, and you never know exactly which city or suburb you're in.

Sidetrip to Jerusalem

The road to Jerusalem from here is nice but becomes more and more difficult as you approach the city. You can take a secondary road through Latrun, where there is a Trappist monastery. The road winds around and gradually climbs. Merge into the main highway as it makes its way through the mountains, through the new suburbs of the city, and finally flattens out as you hit the convention center.

Village on the Left Bank.

Continuation of Route

3. Our tour, however, continues down the coast. I've never figured out how to get around Tel Aviv, but if you keep to the coast you somehow manage to find your way to Ashdod and then to Ashqelon.

4. The distances are not long, and you can ride to Ashqelon in a couple of hours. The coast area is not interesting.

5. At the police station for the entrance to Gaza, you will feel as though you are crossing into another world as you first see the teeming Jabalya refugee camp. The people are friendly as you ride over the sandy and flat area to the Rafah border.

6. The border is not difficult to cross—the Egyptians will stamp a visa in your passport for a small fee—and you can ride on the easy coastal road all the way to Ismaliya and cross the small stretch of water by boat. From Ismaliya, it is not far to Cairo.

Chapter 11
Cyprus

In brief, the island is made up of a Greek Christian majority and a Turkish Islamic minority and is divided into two countries, the Turkish north and the Greek south. It is not possible to cross between the two sides. There is a limited entrance point from the south to the north at Nicosia, a divided city, but you cannot bike both parts of the island in one trip. If your passport shows that you have traveled to the northern part of the island, the Greek Cypriots consider that illegal and won't allow you into the southern half. One way around that restriction is to ask the North Cypriot authorities to stamp a blank piece of paper and place it in your passport.

The people, rather than the land, are what makes this island good for bicycle touring. It's a small country, made even smaller by the fence that divides the two communities, and except for a few stretches, not too scenic. Greek Cyprus is not like Greece, and Turkish Cyprus is not like Turkey. The islanders have their own identity, which is more cosmopolitan and freer then that of their co-linguals in the respective mother countries.

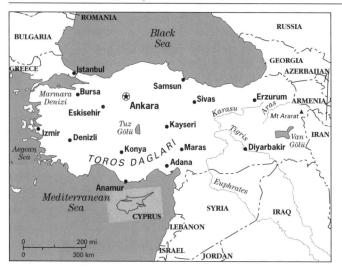

The island is 65 km from Turkey and 100 km from Syria. Each side of the island has its own airport: the old airport near Nicosia which ended up in Turkish hands and receives a limited number of flights, and the airport at Larnaka to which you can get good fares, especially from Athens and Northern Europe. On the Turkish side, ferries operate to Kyrenia (Girne) from Tusucu and Alanya, and to Famagusta (Gazimagusa) to Mersin and Haifa. On the southern side, ferries operate from Jounie (near Beirut), Haifa, Alexandria, Rhodes, Crete, and Pireaus to Limassol. Westerners do not need a prior visa to either side of the island.

Much poorer Northern Cyprus is a bargain, where you can eat a meal for $3 and sleep in a hotel for $5–10, almost as cheap as Turkey. There is a shortage of tourist facilities in the north, and most visitors come by organized tour. The south is more expensive, about the same as Greece, with hotels and restaurants of all categories along the southern coast. People come from surrounding countries to shop in Limassol and Larnaca, as there is an abundance of trade here.

As far as maps go, Freytag & Berndt and Clyde each publish a map that covers Cyprus at 1:250,000 and 1:300,000 respectively and is available in the United States. A reasonably detailed 1:400,000 Visitor's Map of Cyprus is available for free from the Cyprus Tourist Office, or CTO. The tourist office will also give you a detailed map including all the monasteries and Byzantine churches of the Troodos mountain area north of Limassol.

You can fly into the several airports on the island, but the best choice is to arrive by ferry. Ferries are inexpensive on both sides of the island. The hydrofoil from Tusucu costs under $15, including port taxes. A ferry from Rhodes to Limassol is $25–35, and it is at the port city of Limassol that we start our tour.

The difficult part of the country is located at the northern part of Greek Cyprus, where the mountain road climbs to over 1000 m. Most of the rest of the island is rolling hills. Put your rear view mirror on your right, because here we ride on the left and see signs in miles.

Accommodations

Every city in Greek Cyprus is overflowing with hotels. It is best to make reservations beforehand, but outside the peak summer season, you stand a good chance to get in somewhere. In the north there are a few hotels in the main cities.

1. Tour of Cyprus from Limassol

Distance: 150–300 km (93–186 miles)
Terrain: sea shore and dry mountains
Duration: 3–5 days
Rating: very difficult except along the coast

1. Starting at Limassol, travel west on the road to Ypsonas, and just outside the city you come to the Kolossi Castle.

Bicycle tourist rest stop.

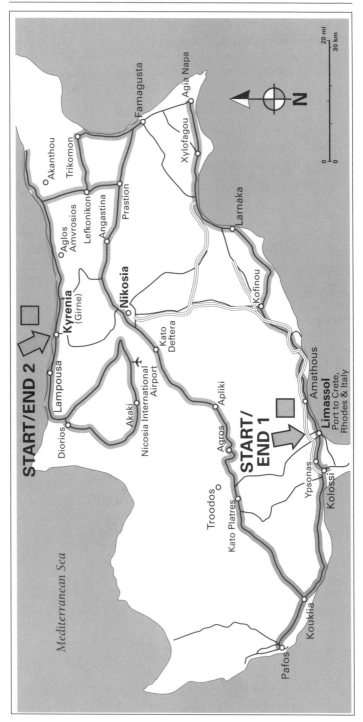

2. Continue around the coast through Kouklia to Pafos, 65 km from Limassol, along the mildly hilly road. Divided into two sections, Pafos is unquestionably the nicest town along the coast. You must see the mosaics at the House of Dionysus and the surrounding ruins. The small Ethnographical Museum is also worth a trip.

3. From Pafos, you can continue north to the northwestern coast with the towns of Polis and Latsi on the Chrysochou Bay, about 50 km farther.

4. Although there is a road that wraps around the island to the north coast, I suggest you backtrack toward Limassol for the next stage.

5. North of Limassol are the the Troodos Mountains with the city of Kato Platres, about 30 km away. This trip involves a steep climb to the center of this mountainy area, from which you can visit the Kykko monastery, the Kaledonia Falls, and Troodos. The entire mountain range is snow-covered in winter. The villages are quaint, with vines over terraces and fellows who stroll around in the evening playing guitars or bouzoukis.

6. From Kato Platres, you can go around to Agros and pass the beautiful village of Kakopetria to the main road to Nikosia.

7. The continuation of the road to Nikosia, 65 km away. Nikosia is a city divided between the north and south, and is not particularly interesting. The old city is the place to be, the museum is a must, and if you need visas for Syria, Jordan, or any other country, this is a good place to get them.

8. The rest of our tour through the Greek part is less stimulating for cyclists, and you won't miss much if you just come to the Troodos mountains and visit Pafos. There are two roads to Larnaka, the old road being a bit quieter. It's an easy road, but it is an arid and empty ride. You can continue around the bay on a flat road to Xylofagou and Agia Napa. These used to be quaint villages, but during the summer they are transformed by masses of tourists. From here, backtrack to the port or the airport.

2. Tour of Northern Cyprus

This region is best reached from Kyrenia (Girne), to where there are ferry services. Most northern cities have two names, one each for pre- and post-occupied Cyprus, so it can become a little confusing.

Distance: 100–200 km (62–124 miles)
Terrain: seashore and dry mountains
Duration: 2–3 days
Rating: moderate

1. After landing at Kyrenia (Girne), turn left and immediately you've exited the small city.

2   Shortly after is Karakum, and next is an intersection where you can continues left to Esentepe or straight to Famagusta (Gazimagusa).

3. Keep left, and 5 km later the coast road changes into a narrow lane. This is a quite hilly, but entirely untrafficked road, and you begin to feel the charm of the area.

4. About 22 km from the port, there's an intersection for Karaagac and 2 km later another intersection for Esentepe, but you want to continue straight. This is one of the most peaceful and lovely rides of our entire trip.

5. You pass the Greenpeace sea turtle protection zone, and it's interesting to go inside and talk to the people. The sea turtles nest in the rocks along the sea.

6. About 40 km from the port, there's a fork for Kantara along the coast or Gecitakale, which leads inland.

7. The short ride to Gecitkale, one of the nicest towns on the island, is quiet and peaceful. There's a 4 km steady climb into a partly wooded area, and then a descent into Gecitkale. It looks on the map like a large city but isn't much more than a village. You can see the signs of war in the bullet-marked buildings.

8. From here it's only 23 km to Famagusta, and from the hills entering the town you can see an expanse of flat land below.

9. I took the lone road to Iskele, which was flat, wide and untrafficked. The road down the coast, slightly inland from the sea, is a bit busier, again flat, but not that exciting.

10. The traffic picks up near Gazimagusa, known by the Greek Cypriots as Famagusta. It's not a large town, and the old part of the city, which includes the Othello Tower, is inside crusader walls. It is said that the city used to have 365 churches, and you will see several in a neglected state. From the port there are now regular ferries to Haifa and Mersin.

11. Ask for directions to the small road for Gonendere. This is a scenic and peaceful road on which you pass a couple of villages along the way.

12. At Cihangir there's a sign for Lefkonikon (Lefkosa). The road continues south and joins the main road.

13. Turn right and continue following the signs for Lefkosa. Unlike the Greek part of this city (altitude 150 m),

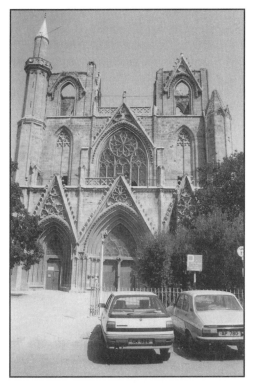

Neglected church in Northern Cyprus.

Turkish Lefkosa is ugly. The military and government have taken over the nicest places.

14. To exit the city, backtrack to the national road for Famagusta and follow the signs for Kyrenia (Girne) and Guzelyurt.

15. The main road across the mountains to Kyrenia is wide with a shoulder. It goes up to about 350 m after a 6 km gradual but steady climb, then has a nice descent.

16. At Turkeli, turn right to Kilicaslan. The road climbs before this intersection but remains gentle to the coast. The flat coastal road takes you to Kyrenia, which has a seaside castle, and from which you can return by ferry.

Chapter 12
Malta

Malta is an island full of Mediterranean history. Everywhere you turn you find either an Arab palace, a crusader fort, or a Phoenician ruin. The smallest country in the Mediterranean, Malta offers a lot to see and I recommend passing 2–5 days there if you can.

The country of Malta consists of three inhabited islands—Malta, Gozo, and Comino. The last is less than 3 km long, and although it has nice beaches, it's not good for cycling. The main island, loaded with history, is Malta, with a length of less than 30 km. Gozo is smaller—17 km at its longest—greener, and more rural. The people are kind, and because of English colonialism, many speak fluent English. The native language is an interesting mix of a dialect of Arabic with words from all over the region.

Malta is less than 100 km south of Sicily, midway between Gibraltar and Port Said. It has a population of less than 350,000. The most popular way to get there for overland travelers is a regular Tirrenia ferry, which runs a couple of times a week from Syracuse. The trip takes five hours and costs about $35. In summer you can find ferries from Catania, Reggio Calabria, and Naples. Malta has a

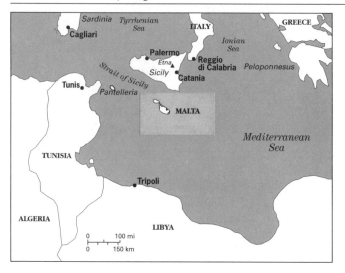

decent international airport which accommodates flights from all major European and North African cities. During May, June, September, and October, you can find good deals on charters from European capitals.

If you're too tired or hot to ride, Malta has a good and inexpensive bus system that links every part of the island. The main bus station is located just outside the city gate of Valletta. Walking is also a good way to see the island. You can pick up a walking guidebook in local tourist stores. Many of Valletta's streets, for example, are staircases, making walking the only logical way to see this historic city. The roads on Malta are well surfaced, wide, and lightly trafficked except around the Valletta-Sliema area; you should have no problem cycling.

As in Cyprus, you ride on the left. Malta is also one of the few places around the Mediterranean that is not hilly. The only hilly area is in the southwest part of the island, south of Rabat, which offers spectacular views of the blue sea from the road perched on cliffs less than 200 m above the sea. There are some smaller cliffs on the southern part of Gozo, but the rest of the riding is flat and easy. Remember that Malta is very far south, just off North Africa, and if you're there during August when a wind is blowing from the Sahara, you will suffer from the extreme heat.

Malta does not have campgrounds or youth hostels, but there are a variety of hotels in the Sliema area and a handful of other hotels along the beaches in other parts of the island.

Although Valletta is the capital, Sliema is the primary city. You can get a cheap hotel for less than $25 a night for two; rates go up from there to deluxe European prices. By and large, Malta is not an expensive place. You can eat lunch for under $5. Malta is a traditional and conservative Roman Catholic country. Although it is by no means uptight, modest behavior is expected.

Much of the history of Malta is war related, so if you're interested in the history of conflict, you'll find many forts and museums to suit your taste. However, the island is also full of grand buildings, quaint old villages, natural beauty, caverns and grottos, and friendly people. A good map of Malta is the 1:50,000 scale map published by Hildebrand.

Accommodations

Apart from many hotels in Sliema, Malta has a few other resorts that can be booked through a travel agent.

1. Tour of Malta

Distance: 100 km (62 miles) and you'll see everything
Terrain: rolling and dry
Duration: 2–5 casual days
Rating: easy

1.1 Valletta to Zabbar

1. Start by passing through the narrow streets of Valletta, an old baroque town built by the Knights of St. John of Jerusalem, who dominated Malta until almost the 19th century. You can spend an entire day roaming the buildings and the stores. The bus station at the Valletta gate is a good place to start your tour.

2. From the bus station, go straight to the Triton Fountain and down St. Anne Street through Floriana until you reach the National Road.

3. Take the road to Marsa, an industrial town, and continue to Paola, which has a few distinctive old buildings.

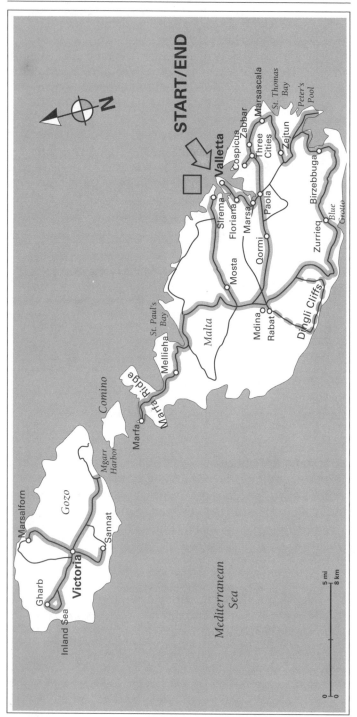

4. Turn left and go up the Corradino Heights until you reach the Three Cities of Vittoriosa, Cospicua, and Senglea.

5. Then follow the signs to Zabbar, another pleasant town, and Marsascala, a quaint fishing village with beaches and places to eat along the water.

1.2 Zabbar to Mdina

1. Go down to St. Thomas Bay—which has more beaches—and turn left past the Mamo Tower to Zejtun. This is another old and friendly town worth touring.

2. Just after the town, a road takes you to the coastal village of Marsaxlokk where the Turkish fleet docked during their attack on the island. If you enjoy jumping into the Mediterranean from rocks, go around the bay about a mile to Peter's Pool.

3. From Marsaxlokk, take the coastal road west through Birzebbuga and then to Zurrieq.

4. If quaint seaside locales are more to your taste, follow the south road to the Blue Grotto, which I consider one of the nicest places on the island.

5. From Zurrieq, take the road through Qrendi and follow it west a few miles and climb to Mdina. This will be the hardest part of a generally easy trip. Also called the Silent City, Mdina is a must for visitors to Malta.

6. Haunting and majestic, Mdina was the capital of the island during Arab rule, when they occupied Malta until the time of the Crusades. There is also a lot to see in Rabat, an extension of Mdina. You can easily spend the afternoon touring the narrow streets and buildings.

Sidetrip to Dingli Cliffs

An optional part of the tour is to go south on the hilly road to the Dingli Cliffs, where you catch a breathtaking and uncluttered view of the blue sea while riding along the high road that parallels the sea.

1.3 Mdina to Mosta

1. From Mdina, you can either ride back to Valletta for the night, or continue west if it is still early in the day. Along the ride between Mdina and Valletta is the quaint town of Qormi which is worth visiting.

2. From Sliema (or straight from Mdina), take the road to Mosta. This too is a typical Maltese city with a large church, St. Mary, capped by an especially large dome. The streets in the neighboring city of Balzan are also worth a ride through.

3. From Mosta, take the road through the Targa Gap to St. Paul and the St. Paul's Beach, a resort area, and follow the signs for the rolling road to Marfa, where you can take the ferry to Gozo.

2. Tour of Gozo

Although Gozo does not have the historical interest of Malta, it is also attractive and interesting.

1. The half-hour Gozo ferry lands at Mgarr, where you will probably be struck by the difference between Gozo and Malta. Myth has it that Calypso kept Ulysses on Gozo for seven years.

2. You can ride directly to Victoria, which local people sometimes call Rabat.

3. From there, the south road takes you south to Sannat and an overview of the cliffs; the north road takes you to the resort area at Marsalforn, probably the most interesting town on Gozo, which has hotels and restaurants. Finally there is a west road, which takes you across farmlands to the sea at Gharb.

Chapter 13
Crete

Crete is an island of mountains and cliffs; even many of the coastal roads are steep and difficult. The northern coast of the island has been spoiled somewhat by tourism, but the people away from the tourist areas are kind and the scenery everywhere is beautiful. The main population center is on the northern part of the island, so you find many peaceful, uninhabited roads on this trip.

The island is served by the airports at Hania, Iraklion, and Sitia. During summer, all three receive flights from many European cities. The island also has five main ports, all on the northern shore: Souda, Rethimno, Iraklion, Agios Nikolaos, and Sitia. There are daily ferries to the island from Pireas as well as ferries from other Greek Islands, Cyprus, Egypt, Israel, and Turkey.

The island has been developed for tourism, so hotels and camping abound. The Greek tourist office is your best source of information about ferry services and hotels and campgrounds. I have chosen a tour that will pass the three most popular ports, with Iraklion as the starting point. The best maps available are those by Ravenstein at 1:250,000 and Freytag & Berndt at 1:200,000.

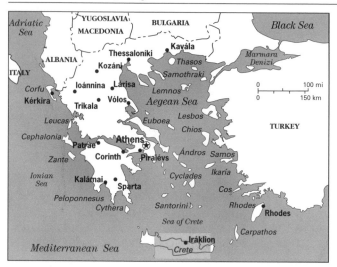

Tour of Crete

Distance: 410 km (256 miles)
Terrain: mountainous
Duration: 3–6 days
Rating: difficult

1. Iraklion to Kasteli via Knossos

Distance: 42 km (26 miles)

1. From Iraklion, which is Crete's main city but not very large, follow the signs for Knossos, going uphill and out of the city.

2. In the urban area, follow the sign for the Knossos antiquities, 3 km.

3. Pass the Nea Alatsata suburb, continue uphill for a km, and descend into Knossos. Many places nearby will keep your bike as you tour the famous reconstructed ruins of the ancient city.

4. Continue along the narrow road, which carries a moderate amount of traffic. As you wind through the barren and beautiful mountains, climb for 2 km.

5. Turn left at the road to Skalani and Mirtia. This quiet road brings you to Skalani in a km, with a great view of

the bay and the hills around. Continue to Mirtia, 5 km, on a rolling road.

6. These are handsome villages, where the dress and the customs are traditional. The first part of this road is the hardest as you ascend to 300 m.

7. Descend to Kasteli, 14 km away. Turn left, and continue the hilly, quiet, and pretty journey. The road surface is a bit bumpy.

8. Go through Apostoli and continue to Kasteli on the eucalyptus-lined lane.

Sidetrip to the Plateau of Lassithi

Distance: 62 km (39 miles)

1. Return to the north coast by following the sign to Limani Hersonissou. The winding and tranquil road is great to ride.

2. Around the 7 km mark is the turnoff to the traditional villages of the Plateau of Lassithi.

3. The road up to Gonies and Tzermiado (27 km) is hard, but around the dozen villages, you cycle on a gently rolling road. It's a lovely area for a sidetrip.

2. Kasteli to Agios Nikolaos

Distance: 58 km

1. The main tour drops down to the sea and passes a large aquatic park at the 5 km mark. You get a lovely view as you gradually descend.

2. Turn right on the National Road, following the sign to Agios Nikolaos, 36 km.

3. Enter Limani Hersonissou, and you'll probably shake your head at its rather crass tourism. This road is fairly busy but mostly flat.

4. You reach the beach community of Stalida at the 166 km mark. From here, there's another inland road that continues to Mohos and the Lassithi plateau.

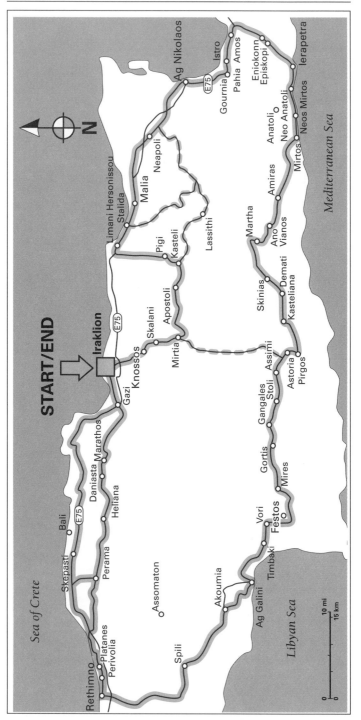

5.   After a small stretch of road, you arrive at Malia and its
     archeological site. Everywhere there are cars,
     motorbikes, and bicycles to rent. The road begins to
     climb as you go inland.

6.   From here you may decide to take the old national road,
     which is longer and more hilly, as an alternate to the
     new main road. For the most part, the two run parallel,
     so both are feasible routes.

7.   After a 5 km climb to about 350 m, the main road has a
     dark tunnel at the 182 km mark before descending.

8.   From Neapoli, the old road may be the better choice
     since it's not as difficult, but both roads continue to be
     hilly through the rugged, empty countryside.

9.   You must take the main road to the attractive town of
     Agios Nikolaos.

3. Agios Nikolaos to Mirtos

Distance: 52 km (33 miles)

1.   Follow the signs for Ierapetra, 35 km away. Climb out of
     the city, take in the lovely view, and continue on the
     curving road along the water.

2.   The small village of Istro, 10 km away, is on this scenic,
     isolated road. You can see the archeological site of
     Gournia from the road as you wind around the gulf.

3.   Descend into Pahia Amos and take the right fork to
     Ierapetra. This lovely town is located in an olive-
     growing area.

4.   Follow the sign for Mirtos, 14 km, on the easy road. At
     first there is a light industrial area with unattractive
     buildings, but after Amoudares you climb for a
     beautiful view between the brown and chalk-colored
     mountains.

4. Mirtos to Gortis

Distance: 88 km (55 miles)

1. The next part is more difficult. Leaving Mirtos, climb for 6 km and look over the sea. This part of the road is especially beautiful as it continues climbing and descending.

2. The top of one hill is at the intersection for Sikologos, where you see a large church to your left.

3. Descend and climb again to the village of Pefkos at almost 600 m. You catch glimpses of the sea through the rocky mountains.

4. Go back down to reach Agios Vassilios. The road continues to roll, and soon you see the pretty town of Ano Vianos nestled in the brown mountains. The road is beautiful but not easy at this point.

5. At the fork, follow the sign for Iraklion. About 8 km later is another fork where you follow the signs for Skinias, 8 km.

6. Go through the town of Martha and continue on a very quiet road surrounded by olive trees. In some places the road surface is rough.

7. Go through Skinias and descend to the small village of Demati, where the road rolls through the plain.

8. Go through Pirgos, a small town, and 5 km later is an intersection that returns to Iraklion on a scenic road or continues to Assimi and Loures. The signs are not very accurate here, so keep your eyes open and ask people for directions.

9. The road is difficult around Gangales. A short time later you come to the archeological site of Gortis. There's a place here to keep your bike.

4. Gortis to Agia Galini

Distance: 30 km

1. Continue to Mires. Go through the town of Mires and follow the signs to Festos (Phaestos). If I had to select two must-see archeological sites on Crete, one would be Knossos and the other Festos.

2. Follow the signs to Festos, and then backtrack to the road to Timbaki. You see signs advertising an ethnology museum at Vori, 2 km off the road.

3. From Timbaki follow the signs for Rethimno, 60 km. Turn right, and after a couple of km you begin to climb steeply for about 3 km on a beautiful road that gives you a glimpse the sea.

4. Descend into Agia Galini, where there's a nice place to camp.

5. Agia Galini to Rethimno

Distance: 61 km (38 miles)

1. Continue to climb until the intersection for Kria, about 400 m altitude, then descend slightly into Akoumia, a nice town with terraced gardens.

2. The road is easy to Spili. You see villages nestled into the mountains along the way. Across the valley is the road from Assomaton cut into the side of a mountain.

3. Descend to an intersection with that road, then continue to climb and descend until about 8 km out of Rethimno. It's a wide, well-paved, and scenic road.

4. The descent into Rethimno is gorgeous. Continue under the highway and follow the coastal route through Perivolia.

5. Go to the old part of town and turn right. The coast road is obvious, and the towns, Perivolia, Missiria, Platanes, and Kambos, make up one long beach scene.

6. Return to Iraklion

Distance: 78 km (49 miles)

1. At Stavromenos at the 68 km mark you must choose to
    stay on the old road or return to the highway. The new
    road, not heavily trafficked, goes along the beach, and
    has rolling hills. The old road brings you inland through
    Perama. Both roads become quite difficult all the way to
    Iraklion.

2. Return to the coastal highway, which is scenic and has
    three long climbs. The first climb takes you to the
    turnoff for Bali. You get a view of the sea and the
    rugged mountains.

3. At the 34 km mark there's a 10% uphill grade, a descent
    to the 24 km mark, and then another 2 km ascent.

4. When you turn toward the Gulf of Iraklion, the hills
    taper off. At Gazi you can exit and take the beach road
    all the way to the center of Iraklion.

Chapter 14
Rhodes, Samos, and Karpathos

These three islands are among the largest in Greece and are good to ride. Most of the information given in Chapter 7 for Greece also applies to these islands. Good information is available from the Greek tourist office, and the maps that cover Greece, such as the recommended series by Freytag & Berndt, cover these islands in adequate detail. Additional maps of the islands are also available from the local tourist offices. Accommodation is plentiful, especially on Rhodes, and you're never far from hotels or camping facilities.

1. Tour of Rhodes

Distance: 182 km (113 miles)
Terrain: coast with some hills
Duration: 2–3 days
Rating: moderate

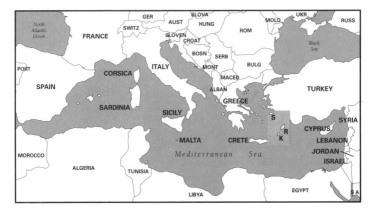

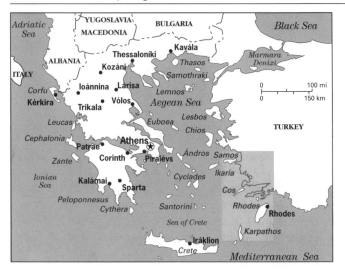

This island gets five stars for bicycle touring. The road around the island is a pleasure to ride, and the islanders are helpful and friendly. The port and airport are near Rhodes city at the top of the island. Flights and ferries to and from Europe and the Middle East are relatively cheap and easily accessible. Spend as much time as you like in pleasant Rhodes city. Accommodation is better in the old city than in the new one.

The island is small, and our simple yet spectacular tour around it is less than 200 km. We are suggesting a circular tour of the island, starting at Rhodes; but if you have less time, you could do just the tour to Lindos and back to Rhodes, which can be done in one day, or in two easy days with an overnight stop in Lindos. For the bigger tour, just continue from Lindos via Apolakia and from there back to Rhodes.

1.1 Rhodes to Lindos

Distance: 47 km (29 miles)

1. Starting outside the walls of the old city, follow the signs for Lindos (47 km) and Faliraki (14 km).

2. Pass the small Rhodes war cemetery, and continue around the beach road through Agia Marina. The road is flat and smooth.

3. Soon the road merges into the main road at Faliraki but never becomes busy. Continue to Afantou. After here the road begins to roll and there's a 3 km hill outside Archangelos.

4. Descend into Arhangelos and get off the road to enter the city. The beaches along the island are nice and can be reached by taking short roads just off our route.

5. There's another 1 km climb near Massari, but generally the road on this side of the island is easy.

6. Take the old road inland. It's a bit longer but not harder than the new road.

7. After Kalathos, follow the sign for Lindos, and climb to where you get a fine overlook of the sea and of the ruins of Lindos. Go into the city and play tourist for a while.

1.2 Lindos to Rhodes via Apolakia

Distance: 135 km (84 miles)

1. When leaving Lindos, continue around the coast to Lardos. There are a couple of short but very steep climbs, and the road surface is not good here.

2. Lardos is a pretty town, and you can take the next intersection into the town if you like. Then backtrack to that same intersection and continue south toward the beach. This road is slightly rolling.

3. As you reach Genadio, there's a sign pointing you to Vation, 7 km. The road climbs steadily through a handsome partly wooded area past Vation to an intersection for Profilia.

4. Take the fork for Apolakia, 7 km away. The last section includes a steep descent. Apolakia is one of the most pleasant towns on the island.

5. The next part of the tour is the only really challenging section. Follow the sign for Monolithos, 10 km, climbing all the way. From here, you get a view over the sea.

6. Climb another km until you're about 350 m, then take it easy to Sianna, another pretty mountain village. The road is moderately difficult for the next few km.

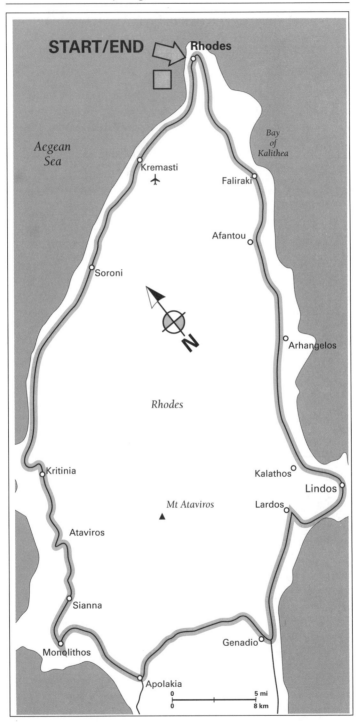

7. Pass the road that goes around the barren Ataviros mountains, and follow the road as it descends into Kritinia.

8. On your right is a castle overlooking the sea as you enter a farming region. The road becomes flat as you ride parallel the isolated beach. There's a marked turnoff for the famous butterfly zone.

9. The rest of the road to the capital is smooth and flat. It gets busy after you pass the airport.

2. Tour of Samos

The islands close to Turkey—Lesbos, Chios, Samos, Kos—are small. Samos is good to ride since we can make a loop around the island in a relaxing day ride. The short ferry from Turkey can take you to Samos. Our tour starts at the port of Samos/Vathi. Accommodation is no problem here either: you can find hotels and camping facilities everywhere.

Distance: 82 km (51 miles)
Terrain: rolling
Duration: 1–2 days
Rating: moderate

1. Climb out of the city and go to Pythagorion, 13 km.

2. There is a 3 km climb followed by a descent into Pythagorion. The road is in decent condition and is lightly trafficked.

3. Continue to Hora, 3 km, then to Pyrgos and across the island to Karlovasi. It is neither a hard nor a long road, but it does have hills before and after Pyrgos. The road is quiet as it passes through rugged terrain.

4. From Karlovasi, the road back to Samos, 30 km away, is an easy, attractive ride along the beach.

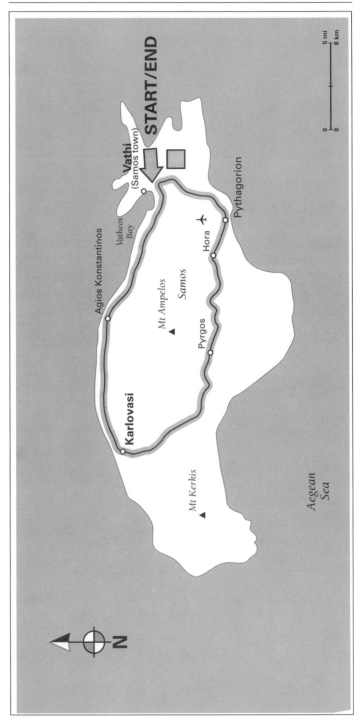

START/END

Vathi
(Samos town)

Vatheos Bay

Agios Konstantinos

Samos

Mt Ampelos ▲

Pyrgos

Hora

Pythagorion

Karlovasi

Mt Kerkis ▲

Aegean Sea

N

5 mi
8 km

3. Tour of Karpathos

You may want to stop in Karpathos because it is on the ferry route between Rhodes and Crete. It is relatively large and less overrun with tourist than the other Greek islands. Karpathos' two regions, north and south, are divided by an unfertile mountain area, and the two cultures developed independently, so in a sense we will be visiting two islands in one. Our tour touches upon most of the villages but only runs about 70 km. Accommodation is a bit more limited, and you can find hotels only in the towns.

Each part of the island has a port, Diafani in the north and Karpathos (also called Pigadia) in the south. The boat from Rhodes first stops at Diafani, where our tour starts. This will be a different disembarking than you are used to since the ferry anchors in mid-harbor while a small motor launch comes alongside and takes you on board. Someone will help you lift your bike into the launch while both the launch and the ferry are gently bobbing in the sea. The northern section of the island is more rustic, and the unmoored entrance gives you a taste of the smallness of Diafani, which has a couple of simple hotels. The north is also more hilly. The nicest beach in the area is at Vananda, where there is a taverna.

Distance: 70 km (44 miles)
Terrain: mountainous
Duration: 1–2 days
Rating: difficult

1. With the help of a steady north wind, head out of town on the road—there's only one—to the impressive village of Olimbos (Elympos), 7 km away. It is a difficult but scenic climb.

2. Olimbos sits on a rocky ridge with large stone windmills along the cliffs. A couple of tavernas along the road offer wonderful vistas. Rest your bike and walk around the quiet city. As in Cyprus and Rhodes, you will see courtyards of white and black stones as well as a variety of shrines around the town. Ask how to get to the Agia Anna chapel, the oldest on the island. There are few tourist facilities in the north, but if you want to stay, ask around for Pension Olimbos.

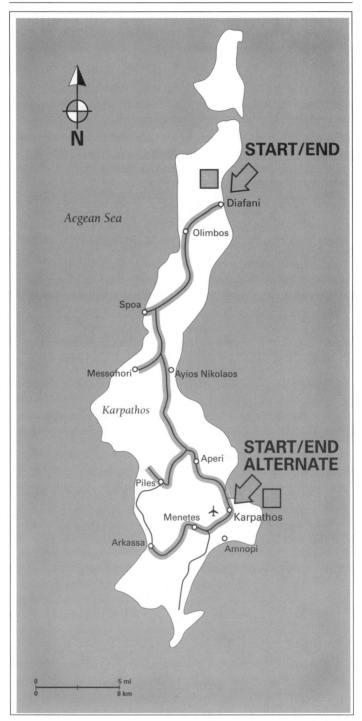

3. When you're ready, head south on the dirt road to the main city of Karpathos, a ride of under 40 km. It is a hilly ride but not very difficult, though the condition of the road is poor. Along the way we will pass a handful of villages.

4. About 10 km south of Olimbos, you can take a a left fork to an isolated pebble beach called Agrios Minas, but remember that you have to climb back up the hill, probably 300 m, to the road.

5. Another 15 km south will bring you to the town of Spoa, a real mountain village. A small road east winds down to Ayios Nikolaos, a partly rocky isolated beach that has a taverna, I Drosseri Akti, and a small shrine.

6. From Spoa you can also go to the western part of the island, but our tour will continue down the east coast, where you will find a few inlets leading to other isolated beaches, including Kira Panagia, which also has a taverna.

7. When you go farther south, you will arrive at a town called Aperi and encounter a hilly paved road. The ancient capital of the city during the Arab conquest, it is a nice place to explore. Visit the house kept in the old style at number 171 on Xrisoxeri Street. The church Kimissis tis Theotokou and the small church Ayios Vassilios are worth visiting, and you can relax at the Eleftheria Kafenion.

8. The road to the right continues up the hill to Othos (500 m), then descends slightly to Piles, a pretty village with flowering gardens. As in the other villages, you can park your bike at the end of the road and walk around inside. Piles has tavernas, stores, and an historic church with fragments of an ancient church in the courtyard.

9. Go back to Othos and down the hill past Volada. This is the best part of the trip as you freewheel on a paved road toward the sea.

10. At the last turn near the power station, ride along a 4 km sandy beach and arrive in Karpathos city. Here you can find several hotels at various rates, or if you intend to stay longer than a few days, ask around and

you will be able to rent a small apartment. I saw people camping near the beach, although there is no designated area. The capital offers diverse activities and has many points of archeological interest. Visitors enjoy spending an evening at Georgios taverna as well as the taverna near Hotel Anesis.

Sidetrips to Arkassa and Menetes

A good trip from Karpathos is to ride over the mountain through Menetes to Arkassa. It's a moderately difficult climb but worth it.

Menetes has a large church also founded on an historic basilica, and if you take a dirt road north you will find the Agis Mammas chapel (Mammas is the saint of shepherds) that has frescoes of the Ascension from the 14th century. While you are in Menetes, stop for a drink at the To Souli taverna.

Arkassa is a spread-out area, which has a good beach as well as hotels and places to eat.

Also from Karpathos there is a well-paved road leading to the airport that passes seaside areas including Amnopi beach, which has a modest hotel.

Chapter 15
Corsica and Sardinia

Sardinia (Sardegna) and Corsica, the smaller island 15 km north, provide some of the best cycle touring in Europe. With their networks of secondary roads, spectacular views of turquoise seas, remote villages next door to exclusive summer villas, these two islands will provide ample interest for weeks of exploration.

The islands' remoteness has given these cultures a unique vitality. Only a generation ago, Sardinia and Corsica were as undeveloped as Central America, with most people tending sheep on the hillsides. Even now after the tourist boom, sheep remains the leading export. Except around the main towns—Cagliari and Sassari in Sardinia, Ajaccio and Bastia in Corsica—there's almost no industry, and both islands are lightly populated.

The city people are as fashionable as anywhere in Italy or France. You see an enigmatic merging of the new and old worlds in towns as well as in the countryside. For cyclists, the lack of both industry and dense population is a welcome

change from the hectic pace of much of continental Europe. The roads are lightly trafficked, except during August when the Italians and French from the continent cram seaside resorts. The sea around the islands remains more unspoiled than anywhere in the Mediterranean.

The two islands, lying south of France and west of Italy, are historically and culturally linked and have their own dialects, but today Corsica is French (a king's wedding present) and Sardinia is Italian. Corsicans have maintained their dialect, which is close to Italian, while most young Sards speak only Italian. Corsica used to be expensive, but that has changed, and prices are now just a bit more than those in France. Sardinia, the second largest island in the Mediterranean, has less than a third of the population of its slightly larger neighbor to the south, Sicily. Much smaller Corsica (about the size of Connecticut) has barely 250,000 inhabitants. Both islands are beautiful.

Corsica's main airports are in Bastia, Calvi, and Ajaccio; those on Sardinia are at Olbia and Cagliari. All receive international flights and inexpensive charters from most European cities. A charter from London to Olbia costs $300 round-trip, while a Paris to Ajaccio charter can be picked up for $250. Meridiana Air has a monopoly on flights from Italy to Sardinia; Rome to Olbia costs about $90 one way. Ferries operate from Marseille, Nice, Genoa, Livorno, Civitavecchia (near Rome), Naples, and Palermo. The main ports on the islands are Bastia, Calvi, Ajaccio, Olbia, and Cagliari. The ferry companies are SNCM, Tirrenia, Corsica Ferries,

NAVARMA, Sardegna Ferries, and the Italian State Railroad (Civitavecchia to Golfo Aranci near Olbia). Cabins need reservations during summer, and some French ferries have eliminated deck class on overnight ships. Bicycles cost a nominal charge. A chair from Nice to Calvi starts at about $60; from Civitavecchia to Olbia expect to pay $30. Rail service on both islands is limited to a couple of lines each, but reliable buses can take you between cities if they have room for your bike.

The best maps for Corsica are IGN sheets 73 and 74 at 1:100,000 or sheet 116 at 1:250,000. Sardinia is covered at scale 1:200,000 by Hildebrand, while the D'Agostini 1:300,000 map of Sardinia will be adequate for most people.

A good way to integrate the two islands with a tour of the continent is to take a ferry to Bastia or Calvi either from the south of France or northern Italy. Then ride south to Bonifacio, cross over to the top of Sardinia by another ferry, and cycle to Cagliari. Finally, take a ferry across to Civitavecchia, Sicily, or Naples. Our tour takes the west road from Calvi to Bonifacio, one of the most beautiful rides in Europe.

1. Tour of Corsica

Distance: 297 km (185 miles)
Terrain: mountainous
Duration: 2–4 days
Rating: difficult

Accommodations

Camping locations are mentioned in the text; hotels are available in all the cities.

1.1 Calvi to Ajaccio

Distance: 160 km (100 miles)

1. Starting at Calvi, which has camping if your ferry arrives late at night, head toward Ajaccio, 160 km away.

2. Start on the coastal road, not the one passing the airport but the D81-b, and climb up a mild hill for the first 5 km.

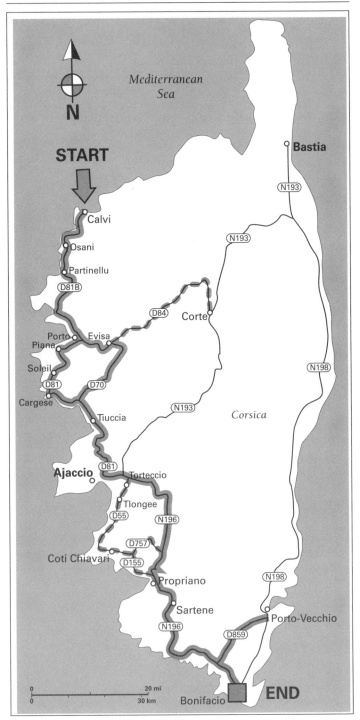

3. Ride on an isolated, rugged road that gives you some spectacular views of the inlets below. The road is narrow and old, with almost no sign of habitation. There's camping after the 14 km marker and a nice beach at 22 km.

4. After a bridge, join the main road, which continues south, and climb 13 km on this narrow road until you look out over 407 m high Col de Palmarella.

5. After more hills on this beautiful road, you reach the small hamlet of Bocca a Croce, a good place to stop. There are a couple of water fountains along the way.

6. Just after 61 km from Calvi, you pass a side road which winds down to the beach at Osani. Partinellu (68 km) is a small village with a couple of stores, a boulangerie, and another road down to the beach. The road has some gentle grades that curve past the sea from time to time; sometimes the water is so clear that you can see people scuba diving.

7. You descend into the pebble beach at Porto (83 km from Calvi), our first real city. It's a lively place, with stores, cafés, a disco, and camping.

8. Cross the bridge, and here you can take the very mountainous D84 inland to Evisa and Corte. If you're a robust cyclist, take this road to see what the natives call the heart of Corsica. It's narrow and winding and very difficult, but it is also very beautiful.

9. Otherwise, turn right after the bridge in the direction of Piana, and climb for a difficult 9 km until you reach about 450 m. There are more drinking fountains along the way and trees to shade you as you pass incredible rock formations.

10. Piana is at the 63 km mark. You will probably not want to take the road down to the beach from the center of town, which is a nice town, unless you want the camping (there's also camping at the 47 km mark).

11. After Piana, the road is a bit wider as it descends toward Cargèse. At the 31 km mark, you arrive at Soleil, a relatively new seaside town. From now on there is camping almost everywhere.

12. Continue along the coast and pass the D70 intersection that goes inland to Vica and Evisa. Although this road is not as hard as the D84, it is much less scenic. The closer to Ajaccio you get, the heavier the traffic will become.

13. Tiuccia, at the 23 km mark, comes next, and there's another beach resort area at the 20 km mark.

14. The last hill before Ajaccio is a 7–8 km tough climb. Descend past a stone aqueduct and enter Napoleon's home town, an antique port city.

1.2 Ajaccio to Propriano

Distance: 83 km (52 miles)

From Ajaccio, many cyclists continue down the N196 main route to Bonifacio, but it has a lot of traffic, including trucks, and is especially narrow and hilly for a main road. I advise the D55, although it is about 10 km longer.

1. First take the N196 out of Ajaccio for about 12 km, and follow the green signs for Bonifacio and Bastia past the airport. This is the busiest and the only unpleasant part of this ride.

2. The southern part of the island is barren and dry, in contrast to the green forested north.

3. At the sign for the D55, turn left, and in 2 km you arrive at Torteccio, a lively hangout for young people.

4. Another 7 km and you pass Tlongee.

5. About 28 km from Ajaccio on this pleasant, easy road, there is a turnoff to Coti Chiavari near a beach camping area. Turn inland here and make a steep 10 km hill through eucalyptus and oak trees. Coti Chiavari, a picturesque village 300 m high, has a beautiful view across the sea of Ajaccio.

6. Continue down the road to Acqua Doria and be alert for another turnoff to the left for Porto Pollo and Propriano, 32 km away. These roads are small and attractive; both solo riders and groups will enjoy them.

7. Go up a very steep 1 km, then proceed to an intersection where you get on the D155.

8. Shortly after, another intersection brings you to the D757. Aways follow the signs for Propriano. Near Propriano you merge into the N196.

9. Propriano, about 83 km from Ajaccio along the coastal road, is a large but peaceful seaside town.

1.3 Propriano to Bonifacio

Distance: 54 km (34 miles)

1. To find the road out of Propriano, ignore the first green sign to Bonifacio; instead, go through the town to the center, and ask someone trustworthy for the road to Sartene. The signs are confusing here, and you'll save yourself a useless hefty climb if you ask for the N196 south.

2. The first part of the road is pleasant and not difficult, but there's a hard 7 km climb to Sartene. I had to walk my bike through the city because one street was especially steep.

3. After Sartene, you have a mixture of up and down roads.

4. At the 103 km mark is a campground, and the road rises again for a couple of km.

5. About 14 km from Bonifacio, there is a turnoff for the D859 to Porto-Vecchio. Porto-Vecchio is a nice city, but the N198 through it has a lot of traffic, more than our N196, which continues on rolling hills.

6. The last part of this road is not as pretty or interesting as the rest, and just when you think you've done the last climb, you see another in the distance, then another. Finally, you arrive at the touristy town of Bonifacio. Across the water you see Sardinia, a 45-minute ferry ride away (it costs about 90 francs with a bicycle).

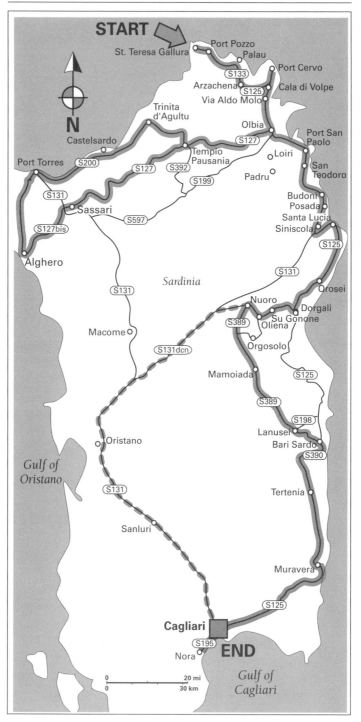

2. Tour of Sardinia

Distance: 414 km (258 miles)
Terrain: mountainous
Duration: 3–6 days
Rating: difficult inland, or moderate if you
                  stick to the coast

Accommodation

When you arrive, go to one of the many tourist offices and get a list of hotels and camping. The nothern part of the island up to Dorgali has many options, but further south there are long empty stretches.

2.1 Santa Teresa to Olbia via Palau

Distance: 70 km (44 miles)

1. Start where the ferry lands in Santa Teresa. Exit the port, go up one block, and turn left on the road through town in the direction of Olbia (60 km) and Palau. Follow the blue signs which in France signify the Autoroute.

2. Generally, Sardinian coastal roads are easier, with fewer climbs, but the real Sardinia, the natives will proudly tell you, lies in the mountains around Nuoro where conquerors couldn't penetrate. If you've climbed hills in Corsica, these will seem easy by comparison.

3. The road to Olbia is somewhat busy and the countryside is rugged. The first part of the road, the S133-b, is mildly uphill. There's camping at Porto Pozzo.

4. At the first intersection 13 km from Santa Teresa, turn left, and a few km later you arrive at an intersection to Palau where you can take a brief optional sidetrip. The town of Palau is not itself that interesting, but it has a ferry to the quaint la Maddalena Island. A bridge from Maddalena connects scenic Caprera Island, where Garibaldi is buried.

5. Back on track, continue down the S133 on a slightly rolling road until you look out over Arzachena, 12 km. Nearby and on other parts of the island, there are prehistoric stone ruins called Nuraghi. To date, no one

has figured out exactly what these large round towers are.

6. About 3 km past Arzachena you see large a furniture store on your right; make a left turn for Porto Cervo.

7. We're going to wind around the loop of the Costa Smeralda because it is both beautiful and famous. The road is slightly hilly, but it yields views of the many coves.

8. You will see a turnoff for Port Cervo, the center of the Costa Smeralda, after about 15 km. It is here that the world's wealthy vacation.

9. Continue around the coast another 5 km until you see a turnoff for Cala di Volpe, and go about 1 km until you come to Cala di Volpe Hotel on your right. This is a wonderful place to explore, but be careful about sitting down and ordering coffee, as it will set you back more than $10—an easy way of keeping the place exclusive.

10. Get back on the main road and follow the signs for Olbia, a flatter road, and after 10 km take the turnoff for Via Aldo Moro, a local road into Olbia, the city with the most active port and airport on the island.

The western part of the island is also attractive. The cities of Castelsardo, which sits on a rock overlooking the sea, and Alghero, a pretty seaside town where the denizens speak Castilian, and Sassari, the main town are especially nice. Port Torres has limited ferry services.

2.2 Olbia to Dorgali

Distance: 113 km (70 miles)

1. If you want to go in that direction from Olbia and make a circle around the island, do not take the main road to Sassari that starts near the airport. Part of it is narrow and winding, with heavy truck traffic. Instead, follow the signs to Tempio Pausania on the S127, then go up the coast from there through Trinita d'Aguto.

2. Another bad stretch of road is the first 25 km of the S125. Maps tell you that there is a main road next to it, what they call the *superstrada*, but it probably won't be

ready before the year 2000, so this narrow winding road is heavily trafficked until just after San Teodoro. Unfortunately, the alternative via Loiri and Padru down the coast is twice as long and five times as hard.

3. When you arrive at Port San Paolo, turn left to the port and enjoy a view of Tavolara Island. You'll find camping nearby as well as in San Teodoro (where there is a 4 km sand beach), Budoni, and near Posada, a city dominated by a tower that you reach by foot from the center of town.

4. The road remains mildly rolling and quiet to Siniscola (55 km from Olbia), an interesting city were the old women still dress in their traditional fringed black and the men sit around the piazza. Roam the narrow streets and you'll be surprised to see Milan-quality clothing shops.

5. There are a couple of roads to Santa Lucia on the coast, but they're not marked so you have to ask. From here continue along to Orosei, 28 m, on a pretty seaside road.

6. After Orosei you pass a marble quarry, and the road turns hilly. It's a 20 km mildly tough climb to Dorgali through a mixture of barren hills and farmland. At 300 m, Dorgali is the only city in the area that has tried to cash in on its traditional atmosphere by opening tourist shops and pizzerias.

7. We are going to continue inland, but if you do not want to do the difficult mountain road that is ahead, which is understandable, then continue down the S125, which remains a gently rolling road. The following roads are bare, with almost no traffic or signs of life between villages.

2.3 Dorgali to Cagliari

Distance: 256 km (160 miles)

1. From Dorgali, backtrack to the main road and follow the sign to Oliena, 18 km, another traditional town. The first part of this quiet road is not bad, but the last 6 km are steep.

2. Along the way there's a turnoff for Su Gonone, a beautiful spring.

3. From Oliena, we have more climbing to reach Nuoro, 8 km. This capital of the province has an interesting costume museum and a nice old section of town.

4. You have to go to the other side of town near the telephone company to pick up the road to Orgosolo; the first part of the road descends, and the rest is rolling.

5. Then head to Mamoiada. There are other mountain roads to various villages, but we're going to drop back to the coast, so get on the main road, the S389, and turn left for Lanusei on another lonely road. From there continue to Bari Sardo, and we're again on the S125, the *strada orientale*.

6. Back on the S125, continue south. The maps show it as a large road, but it has very little traffic. There is a hill area before Villaputzu, but nothing hard.

7. After Muravera you get a good view of the sea, then the road goes inland toward Cagliari (120 km from Bari Sardo), and it's mostly flat. It's a good ride until you come close to the traffic around the Cagliari area.

Cagliari itself is a nice town. From here there are Tirrenia ferries to Palermo, Naples, and Civitavecchia. If you are interested in archeology, visit the ruins at Nora (35 km) across the Stagno and off the S195 down the coast.

Chapter 16
Sicily

Occupying a central position in the Mediterranean, Sicily has been a prime target for conquerors and adventurers. It used to be said that those who control Sicily control the Western world. The culture here is profound. You see this as you pass an open-air market and notice the variety of foods for sale. The island is rich in history, art, music, and literature. In the past century this large island has encountered economic problems and is now one of the less developed regions of an otherwise industrial country. Agriculture remains the livelihood for many, and they produce high-quality goods. Several cities have run-down sections, and the unemployment rate is double the national average, although statistics in Italy are always unreliable since so many people cheat to avoid taxes.

For the touring cyclist, Sicily is a terrific place to ride, a mixture of natural beauty, cities of all sizes, farmlands, and a 3320 m high smoking volcano near the sea. Roads are good, some heavy with traffic but others quiet, with varying degrees of difficulty.

Most Americans associate Sicily with the Mafia. This is not the forum to give a history of the Mob, which in itself is

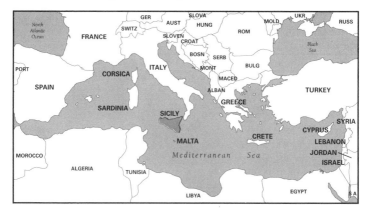

hard to define, but as a visitor you will not notice its presence unless you look hard and see perhaps that a town has only one hotel while it has need of several more, or you see a bunch of factory workers sitting idle. The tentacles of the Mafia have touched the highest strata of the Italian government, and its investments in legitimate businesses in northern Italy as well as overseas make it difficult to isolate. It has been an integral part of Sicilian society with a strict code of conduct, although this has been corrupted in the last decades by the Mafia's commanding position in the international drug market. During times of territorial wars between the various gangs, the Mafia was killing a couple of people a day, but you will not be among them; in fact some argue that the Mafia makes it safer for tourists.

The main ferry service from the mainland at Villa San Giovanne goes to Messina (the lack of a bridge over the narrow strait is another sign of the Mafia's presence). Other ferries reach the island's ports of Palermo or Trapani from Sardinia, Naples, and Tunis, and there is a ferry from Syracuse to Malta. The main airports near Catania and Palermo have flights from several European cities, but bargain fares are difficult to find. Costs here are equal to the rest of Italy, with numerous campgrounds and hotels along the coast. Some of the resorts are crowded and expensive during August. There is a large variety especially on the north and east coast. When you go inland, you need to stop at a town to find a hotel.

The maps to use for your tour of Sicily are from the same series as described in Chapter 2 for Italy. If you choose the d'Agostini 1:250,000 scale regional maps, available in the United States, you only need sheet 17.

Tour of Sicily

Our ride is quite beautiful. Most of it is on the coastal roads that surround the island, but we'll go inland. Roads are good quality, the most popular cycling road being the Palermo-Messina coastal ride, beautiful and mostly easy, though it does suffer from traffic between Palermo and Cefalú and in sections where the Autostrada is incomplete.

The description is based on the assumption that you will be arriving at Palermo. If instead you arrive by ferry from the mainland at Messina, proceed to Section 2 (Messina to Syracuse) first, and save Section 1 (Palermo to Messina) for the conclusion of your tour of the island.

Distance:	794 km (496 miles)
Terrain:	coastal roads with some hills
Duration:	6–10 days
Rating:	moderate, with a few taxing hills

1. Palermo to Messina via Termini

Distance: 251 km (156 miles)

1. If your arrive at Palermo port, either from Sardinia or Tunis, turn left and follow the blue signs for Termini, which will wind you through Palermo's streets and bring you to the coast. Palermo has neighborhoods where you should be careful of your possessions, but it also has beautiful avenues and historic palazzos.

2. The Autostrada takes most of the traffic, while our S113 is flat to gently hilly with a liberal number of hotels and camping, passing lush gardens overlooking the sea.

3. At Ficarazzi (12 km) you have the choice of going around the peninsula to Aspra and Porticello, a slightly hilly but highly scenic ride, or staying on the road through Bagheria, a Mafia stronghold.

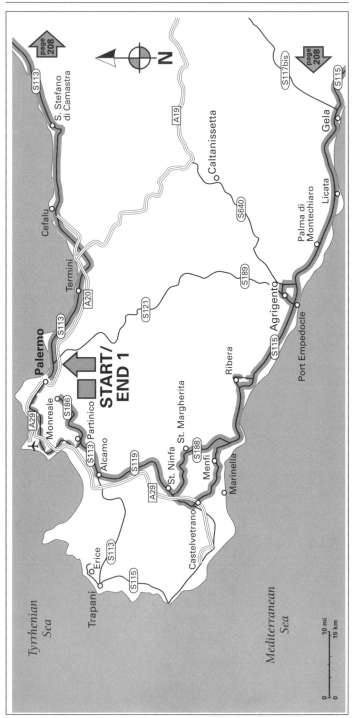

4. Continue through the coastal communities to Termini (37 km), an industrial as well as historic city.

5. Stay on the easy and scenic S113 to Cefalu (67 km), a most popular tourist city with an overwhelmingly solid Norse cathedral, then climb the hill and continue on the road to Messina, another 184 km away at this point. The road is wide where it is busy.

6. You pass San Stefano di Camustra, Sant'Agata di Militello, Brolo, Patti, and the ruins of Tindare, hitting mild hills, then you will find a climb that brings you over 300 m before reaching Falcone.

7. Soon after, you have the choice of continuing through Barcellona or going north to Milazzo (7 km) which has ferry service to the unspoiled Lipari Islands.

8. When the S113 returns to the coast, you pass several pleasant beach communities on a road that is busy in August, but the pretty part of this ride is west of Barcellona.

9. Just after Villafranca Tirrena, you can continue on the 113-dir., which takes some hills and a rough seashore.

10. Also nice is the 5.5 km moderately hilly road to Santa Luca del Mela. If you do not go around, cut over the mountains on the main road, where you have about 10 km of climbing before descending into Messina. Keep going straight, and you will see the port. Few people hang out in Messina for very long, so you may want to continue straight to Taormina from here.

2. Messina to Syracuse via Taormina and Catania

Distance: 188 km (117 miles)

1. From the port, turn south following the blue signs to Catania and Taormina. The ride down this coast is pleasant and light, with only minor hills, mainly around Catania.

2. The first half of the road is touristy, passing one vacation center after another as the road winds through an array of shoreline and city streets. In August it seems

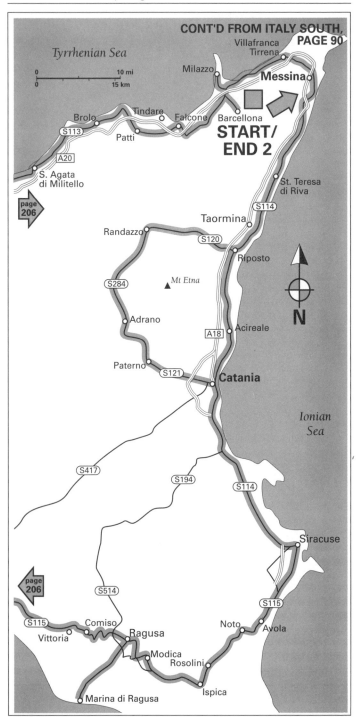

as if half of Europe has come to drive on this volcanic, earthquake-prone strip.

3. It's easy to lose track of which town you are in, and there are a couple of tight turns where you need to be careful, but when you get to the turnoff for Taormina, take the 2 km hill into this grand resort. With its ancient theater and a volcanic backdrop, a continuously moderate climate and exclusive clientele, you would expect hotels and restaurants to be expensive, but quite reasonable accommodation is available in Taormina.

4. Return to the coast, and at Fiumefreddo you can get away from the traffic on the S114 and take a smaller coast road through Riposto and Acireale, which sits on 160 m of warm lava.

5. There are several roads to the foot of smoking Etna, including the difficult and trafficked S120 through Randazzo, and the road to Zafferana, also a climb. Since its last eruption in 1992, which almost wiped out Zafferana, some of the roads and the cable car have been closed, and you need to ask the tourist office at Taormina for updated information on this active volcano. Etna is a humbling and potentially dangerous mountain; you should be sure of yourself, informed, and have warm clothing before attempting to ride it.

6. Farther south on the S114, after the Acireale thermal resort, you will see the island of the Cyclops, then merge into the intense and aggressive traffic of Catania. If you stay on the road near the sea, you pass the train station and the port near the historic city center. Do not stray into the poorer sections of the city. There are some hotels on the way to the airport, but finding accommodation in the city is not easy.

7. Find Via Kennedy and the signs to Siracusa (Syracuse). Although a main road, it is wide, smooth, and lightly trafficked, ruined only by a concentration of polluting industries.

8. Once one of the most potent cities of the ancient world, deserving a generous visit to its historic sights, the compact Syracuse now seems to be in a state of declining grandeur.

3. Syracuse to Agrigento

Distance: 230 km (143 miles)

1. From Syracuse, turn inland on the S125 to Avola, and encounter even less traffic.

2. After Avola, the road climbs to the baroque city of Noto (32 km from Syracuse) and take an up-and-down road to Rosolini.

3. The road slightly climbs to Ispica, then there is a steady climb to Modica (get off the road and go through the lower and upper city) and two winding hilly roads to medieval Ragusa (the M115 is better), over 600 m above the sea. We are now in a different Sicily than the touristy coast, although you can drop to the coast at Marina di Ragusa, rough and scenic, with camping locations.

4. The ride across to Gela on the south coast is fast and fun on a surprisingly lightly trafficked road off-season, over a plateau that yields spectacular views of the sea. There is a steep, winding descent to Comiso near an important and controversial NATO base.

5. The road to Agrigento is straight, dry, slightly lonely, and easy to ride. You pass Gela and Licata, which are neither pretty nor good for swimming.

6. Two km after Palma di Montechiaro, there is a local hilly road that bypasses two long unlit tunnels. I suggest taking the tunnels but using caution and a light, then 3 km later turning left on the local road marked for Cannetello, which leads to the impressive Valley of the Temples at Agrigento, a highlight of the Sicily tour.

7. At Port Empedocie, close by, is a ferry to the island Lampedusa, the southernmost point of Europe.

8. When you're finished visiting the sights, continue to the modern town of Agrigento, home of Pirandello, which is also pleasant.

4. Agrigento to Palermo

Distance: 150 km (93 miles)

1. From Agrigento, continue west on the S115 to Sciacca. You can follow the sign for Eraclea Minoa, 4 km off-road, for lovely isolated ruins. Ribera is 3 km off the road and worth the visit.

2. The S115 is mildly up-and-down. Since we have stayed so long on the coast, I thought we would return inland over the hills to Palermo. The drawback to this is missing Selinute and the easy to ride west coast, including the mystical town of Erice (a hard, steep climb).

3. But let us go north now to Castelvetrano through farmland. You can take either the new S115 past Menfi, a town destroyed by a recent earthquake, 2 km off the road, and Sciacca, an ancient spa (get off the road and ride downhill into town), or the S188. The former passes through interesting farmland.

4. To take the S188, follow the sign to Santa Margherita and then the signs for Castelvetrano at San Bartolo. Both roads are slightly hilly, the serious hills coming after

One of the spectacular temples at Agrigento, which was at one time a major center of Greek culture.

Castelvetrano on the S119, which paralls the Autostrada and goes through San Ninfa.

5. The road to the north coast is hilly all the way, but it is not a long distance. There are no hotels or camping.

6. Pass through the rough countryside until you reach the agricultural town of Alcamo, where you have the choice of picking up the S113 to Partinico or the S186 to Monreale. Although there is scenery along the latter route, especially at Monreale which overlooks the Palermo bay and has an incredible cathedral, it is a hard one to ride. From here, continue to Palermo proper and its ferries.

7. The alternative is to follow the signs to the airport and continue along the S113 around the coast and back into sprawling Palermo, passing several well-to-do communities. To reach the airport from Monreale instead, go west on the A29 or along the minor inland road via Carini.

Appendix: List of Addresses

Sources of maps and travel books

Adventure Cycling Assoc.
PO Box 9308
Missoula, MT 59807

Alpenbooks
3616 South Road C-1
Mukilteo, WA 98275
U.S.A.

American Cycling Publications
6425 Capitol Ave, Suite F
Diamond Springs, CA 95619
U.S.A.

Cordee Books
3A De Montfort Street
Leicester LE1 7HD
Great Britain

Cyclist's Touring Club
69 Meadrow
Godalming, Surrey, GU7 3HS
Great Britain

Fietsvakantiewinkel
Spoorlaan 19
3445 AE Woerden
Netherlands

MapLink
25 E. Mason Street
Santa Barbara, CA 93101
U.S.A.

Sunbelt Publications
1250 Fayette Street
El Cajon, CA 92020
U.S.A.

Commercial Cycling Tour Operators

American Youth Hostels Assoc.
Dept. 806
PO Box 37613
Washington, DC 20013
U.S.A.

Backroads Travel
1516 - 5th Street
Berkeley, CA 94703
U.S.A.

Bike Quest
PO Box 332
Brookdale, CA 95007
U.S.A.

Butterfield & Robinson
70 Bond Street
Toronto, ONT M5B 1X3
Canada

Euro-Bike Tours
PO Box 40
DeKalb, IL 60115
U.S.A.

Open Road Tours
1601 Summit Drive
Haymarket, VA 22069
U.S.A.

Woman Trek
PO Box 20643
Seattle, WA 98102
U.S.A.

Organizations in countries of the region

France:
Féderation Française de
Cyclotourisme
8 rue Jean Marie Tego
75013 Paris

Israel:
Israel Cycling Association
45 Katznelson Street
Givatayim 53216

Italy:
Bici e Dintorni
Borso Reg. Margher 52
10152 Torino

Touring Club Italiano
Corso Italia 10
Milano

Jordan:
Ministry of Tourism
Box 224
Amman

Spain:
Amici de la Bici
Apartad de Correus 10012
08080 Barcelona

Turkey:
Ministry of Culture and Tourism
Gazi Mustafa Kemal Bulvari 33
Demirtepe, Ankara

Bibliography

Listed here are some general travel and cycling books that deal with this area and are useful for additional background information, and cycling books that should help you prepare for international cycle touring.

Mediterranean Europe. Hawthorn, Australia: Lonely Planet, 1995.

Mediterranean Europe Phrasebook. Hawthorn, Australia: Lonely Planet, 1993.

Middle East on a Shoestring. Hawthorn, Australia: Lonely Planet, 1994.

Bicycle Touring in the 90s. Emmaus, PA (U.S.A.): Bicycling Magazine, 1992.

Murphy, Dervla. *Full Tilt.*London: John Murrey, 1965; Arrow, 1987

Nasr, Kameel. *Bicycle Touring International*. San Francisco: Bicycle Books, 1992.

Savage, Barbara. *Miles from Nowhere*. Seattle: Mountaineers, 1983.

Selby, Bettina. *Riding to Jerusalem*. Glasgow: Sidgewick and Nelson, 1985.

Van der Plas, Rob. The Bicycle Touring Manual. San Francisco: Bicycle Books, 1993.

——. *Roadside Bicycle Repair*. San Francisco: Bicycle Books, 1995.

Index

Other Titles Available from Bicycle Books

Title	Author	US Price
All Terrain Biking	Jim Zarka	$7.95
The Backroads of Holland	Helen Colijn	$12.95
The Bicycle Commuting Book	Rob van der Plas	$7.95
The Bicycle Fitness Book	Rob van der Plas	$7.95
The Bicycle Repair Book	Rob van der Plas	$9.95
Bicycle Repair Step by Step (color)*	Rob van der Plas	$14.95
Bicycle Technology	Rob van der Plas	$16.95
Bicycle Touring International	Kameel Nasr	$18.95
The Bicycle Touring Manual	Rob van der Plas	$16.95
Bicycling Fuel	Richard Rafoth	$9.95
Cycling Canada	John Smith	$12.95
Cycling in Cyberspace	Kienholz & Pavlak	$14.95
Cycling Europe	Nadine Slavinski	$12.95
Cycling France	Jerry Simpson	$12.95
Cycling Great Britain	Hughes & Cleary	$14.95
Cycling Kenya	Kathleen Bennett	$12.95
Cycling the Mediterranean	Kameel Nasr	$14.95
Cycling the San Francisco Bay Area	Carol O'Hare	$12.95
Cycling the U.S. Parks	Jim Clark	$12.95
A Guide to Cycling Injuries*	Domhnall MacAulley	$12.95
In High Gear (hardcover)	Samuel Abt	$21.95
The High Performance Heart	Maffetone & Mantell	$10.95
The Mountain Bike Book	Rob van der Plas	$10.95
Mountain Bike Maintenance (color)	Rob van der Plas	$10.95
Mountain Bikes: Maint. & Repair*	Stevenson & Richards	$22.50
Mountain Biking the National Parks	Jim Clark	$12.95
Roadside Bicycle Repair (color)	Rob van der Plas	$7.95
Tour of the Forest Bike Race (color)	H.E. Thomson	$9.95
Cycle History – 4th Intern. Conference Proceedings (hardcover)		$30.00
Cycle History – 5th Intern. Conference Proceedings (hardcover)		$45.00

Buy our books at your local book store or bike shop.

If you have difficulty obtaining our books elsewhere, we will be pleased to supply them by mail, but we must add $2.50 postage and handling, or $3.50 for priority mail (and California Sales Tax if mailed to a California address). Prepayment by check or credit card must be included.

Bicycle Books, Inc.
1282 - 7th Avenue
San Francisco, CA 94122, U.S.A.
Tel.   (415) 665-8214
FAX (415) 753-8572

In Britain: Bicycle Books
463 Ashley Road
Poole, Dorset BH14 0AX
Tel.   (01202) 71 53 49
FAX (01202) 73 61 91

---

* Books marked thus not available from Bicycle Books in the U.K.